REA ACPL ITEM

3 1833 00165 3

DISCARDED

SO-ATG-186

2

GRIFFIN, Robert F.   0831

THE CONTINUING CONVERSATION

**DO NOT REMOVE
CARDS FROM POCKET**

ALLEN COUNTY PUBLIC LIBRARY

FORT WAYNE, INDIANA 46802

You may return this book to any agency, branch,
or bookmobile of the Allen County Public Library.

OEMCO

the Continuing Conversation

Fr. Robert F. Griffin, C.S.C.

Our Sunday Visitor, Inc.
Huntington, Indiana 46750

ACKNOWLEDGMENTS: This work is a collection of a number of the author's columns appearing in *Our Sunday Visitor* weekly magazine. Except for some minor changes, the columns have been reprinted here as they originally appeared in the *Visitor*. Scripture texts used in this work are taken from the *New American Bible,* © 1970 by the Confraternity of Christian Doctrine, Washington, D.C., and are used by license of said copyright owner. No part of the *New American Bible* may be reproduced in any form without permission in writing from the copyright owner. All rights reserved.

Allen County Public Library
Ft. Wayne, Indiana

Copyright © 1985 by Our Sunday Visitor, Inc.
All rights reserved.

With the exception of short excerpts for critical reviews, no part of this book may be reproduced in any manner whatsoever without permission in writing from the publisher. Write:
Our Sunday Visitor, Inc.
200 Noll Plaza
Huntington, Indiana 46750

International Standard Book Number: 0-87973-828-6
Library of Congress Catalog Card Number: 85-80352

Cover design by James E. McIlrath

PRINTED IN THE UNITED STATES OF AMERICA

828

John Reedy, C.S.C.
(1925—1983)

7090831

As editor of the *Ave Maria* magazine, Father John Reedy was always asking me to write articles for him. As the publisher at Ave Maria Press, he kept urging me to give him a book to publish. A year or so before his death, he wanted to see the file I kept of my published essays. I told him I had given up keeping copies of anything I wrote, because I didn't have room for them. He shook his head in disbelief, saying: "I never heard of anyone writing as much as you do who didn't keep copies."

He kept his own file on me and spent months gathering material which he hoped to see published as a book. By the time he finished, he was seriously ill, and we had run out of time. His effort was his final gift of encouragement to me as a writer. I'm so grateful for his attention. He made me feel that my work was very personal to him.

I dedicate *The Continuing Conversation* to the memory of John Reedy, hoping that it is the kind of book he would have published if he had lived. For over two decades, he kept me excited about writing. Trusting his honesty, I persevered to please him. I owe him more than I can ever explain. I want this book to be his book as well as my own, feeling he would be patient with its faults. Patience was so much a part of the love he showed me in the continuing conversation that went on between us. He would be pleased that Bob Lockwood and Our Sunday Visitor did something for me that he wanted to do himself.

Contents

CHAPTER 1

The Continuing Conversation

Hemingway's Santiago, the old man of the sea, has been interpreted as a secular Christ-figure. Suffering wounds in his hands and back, he struggles heroically to catch the great fish, which he addresses as his brother. Having conquered the marlin, he takes his catch back to port while battling sharks which tear destructively at the fish until they have devoured it.

On land again, Santiago carries the mast from his boat up the hill, falling once or twice under the weight of it. In his shack, he falls asleep with outstretched arms under a picture of the Sacred Heart. He will fish on another day, after he has rested. With his courage and endurance, he is a moral victor undefeated by his great disappointment as a fisherman.

Hemingway has a play in which a Roman centurion, present at the crucifixion, says of Christ: "He was pretty good in there today." In the ordeal which tested him, Santiago was pretty good. He was a hero as Christ was a hero. Hemingway was not writing a parable on the redemption of the world. Hemingway was asked if he intended to attach symbolism to his story. He answered: "I knew that if I wrote about a real old man and a real fish and a real boat, it would mean something important to somebody." This, more or less, is what Hemingway said about the symbolism of *The Old Man and the Sea*.

Hemingway's answer helps me explain why I write as I do. If I can speak truthfully of my life, maybe it will mean something to somebody. Wherever I have been, in this enormous struggle with existence, you have been there too. The best, as well as the worst, are sinners redeemed by grace. You can't win them all, the saying goes. On the best days, we win more than we lose; on the worst days, we count our failures and offer them to Jesus, who will make them glorious.

Writing, for me, is the continuing conversation on the pain and happiness we all know about, in the hope that it will help you. I enjoy the books of John Updike. He tells me of ordinary, sometimes earthy things I have noticed, and wondered or worried at, but was too shy to ask questions about. Continuously, he offers me little shocks of recognition by which I see myself in the humiliations or successes of my brother, who chemically, biologically, and poetically gives me back a mirror image of myself.

I am no Updike. I'm a pilgrim in a world that is parceled out between God and the devil. The devil, as the spoiler, messes up our most holy endeavors; yet even the devil's worst mischief — like wars and famines — has its champions of grace, like Mother Teresa or Father Bruce Ritter. As a pilgrim, I'm everything but a saint — remote like a star, yet not altogether a castaway living without a clue. I'm on the lookout for evidence, the intimations of immortality.

Reading Genesis and Exodus, I've become very fond of the God of the patriarchs: He is greathearted, compassionate, and long-suffering, mercifully accommodating himself generation after generation to the willful, alienating, ever-increasing self-centeredness of the children of Adam. Abraham, Moses, and Jacob had their moments of greatness, but Yahweh is plainly their superior in greatness. The biblical accounts give me confidence in the Holy Spirit as scriptwriter. Human authors could not make God in His magnificence so believable and lovable. Even Milton, writing *Paradise Lost*, failed to make Christ as vivid with His compassion as Satan was with his rebellion.

A commentator suggests that St. Paul, writing from prison and thinking of death, betrays anxiety. Dealing with death in the abstract, Paul is always confident with his scenario of the resurrection. As death pushed near, because martyrdom was possible, Paul's lyricism missed a beat as he put the evidence together for his faith. The text does not give much support to this opinion, but I wish it did. I would feel so close to him if he let his doubts show through. I love St. Paul, at his very best in writing hymns and doxologies. He was a believer who never hesitated. I'm closer to the patriarchs who show us gaps in their faith. Jacob spent the night wrestling with God. How strange to read that he had the physical strength which nearly defeated God. Why would God want to arm-wrestle with a patriarch? The Testaments leave us with unanswered questions. Perhaps it wasn't easy to be a patriarch.

A letter-writer tells me I will not attract vocations if I write about things as disedifying as drinking. Perhaps, too, couples will be discouraged from attempting fidelity after reading Updike on marriage. I trust Updike, as a

3

writer, though I don't always like what he says. If I wanted to know how perfect marriage should be, I would read the marriage ceremony.

Perhaps you think I am writing to show that priests are human: they sweat, and get gas on their stomachs, and waste time watching the tube. It would be redundant to say that priests are human, for God has not ordained angels to preach His Gospel. Bernanos's country priest as he is dying says it is not necessary for him to receive the Eucharist because "Grace is everywhere." The French could be also translated as "Everything is grace." The image suggests to me a world crumbling into disappointment at our fingertips; wiping off the dust, we are amazed to see our hands powdered with gold.

The young Catholic bothered by my attending a social hour would probably be bothered by the way I say Mass, though I try to be very careful the way I say Mass. I try to be nearly as careful in eating an hors d'oeuvre. According to the theology of the religious life, there are graces waiting at a happy hour that are unavailable for the rest of the day. Brothers come together socially to do something as neutral as eating and drinking. In being present to one another, they create a chemistry which mediates love. We are spirit-filled creatures doing secular things, not secular creatures who become Christians in doing holy things like saying the office. Grace is everywhere, even in rectories; there are no activities inappropriate to grace, even when the pastor is playing golf.

Once, I asked the late Father John Reedy: "Why do we write?" He answered humblingly, "Because of our egos." I know myself as a center of consciousness watching the mills of the gods grinding slowly. I am aware of the visible world which, if I touch it, touches back. There

4

is also an invisible world which shapes in love the tangible kindnesses and beauty. The beauty is elusive like the lost childhood, and I'm on my guard against the thief. Sometimes the thief looks like God, stern as a schoolmaster. Sometimes he is the archenemy, the thief of paradise.

Some days there is no thief to blame but myself, giving away the treasure that belongs to the house. Ego makes me want to play one of the spies who report on the enemy. Updike, listening like a bug on the bedroom walls of suburbia, writes novels tattling marital gossip. This private center of consciousness, the priest at his typewriter, goes on a weekly ego trip, an Updike of a peeping Tom, as curious as a church mouse nibbling incense, at home among all things visible, like the novena crowd, and invisible, like the faith that moves mountains, of which the Sunday creed speaks.

Hemingway wrote a story about the old man and the sea, which won the Nobel prize for literature. He could have written an epic of the whaling industry, like Melville. He could have sent Santiago on a raft down the Mississippi, like Huckleberry Finn. He only wrote a novelette about a codger who could be Jesus Christ Superstar or the old man praying "Our *nada* who art in *Nada*, *Nada* be thy name. . ." (from "A Clean, Well-lighted Place"), *nada* being the Spanish word for "nothing."

Moby Dick and *Huckleberry Finn* were ideas whose time had come. Hemingway had a different idea when he wrote his story. An egocentric priest could write columns about social justice or the appearance of Our Lady. St. Paul didn't want to preach the Gospel in cities where other missionaries had preached it before him. In journalism, as in evangelism, there is no need of chewing the same cabbage twice. I try to serve social justice

5

when I describe the street people during summers in New York. My dog Darby O'Gill II was Our Lady's gift to me, standing in a grotto drenched with moonlight praying that the original Darby, old and sick, would make it back from the valley of death. Darby II is a more personal miracle than the healings at Fatima.

An English professor on campus thinks that John Updike's talents were wasted in writing the three novels about Harry "Rabbit" Angstrom. "Rabbit is not a character worth developing," the professor feels. The biblical writer of Genesis chose a graceless theme describing Noah, drunk and naked, made fun of by his youngest son. Perhaps the writer perceived a truth, now lost sight of, which he could pass on in no other way, just as Hemingway and Updike had to pass on their insights in the form of human shapes being heroic or shabby.

The continuing conversation will not be enjoyed by everyone who listens. It is embarrassing to be a long-winded monologist. It's only the ego that keeps me going. For a city priest, as for a country priest, everything feels like grace.

CHAPTER 2

Views From A Wet Blanket

I stood with an old priest, watching while the maintenance crew took down a diseased elm.

"Did you ever read Chekhov's play *The Cherry Orchard?*" the priest asked.

"It used to be a favorite of mine," I said.

"The death of the trees symbolized the end of an age," he said. "In the final scene, you hear the sounds of axes cutting down the cherry orchard."

Buzz saws whined as they amputated branches.

"We've lost a number of our Dutch elms in recent years," he said. "Their departure leaves lonely stretches against the sky."

"Nothing else changes," I said. "We put up new buildings. The lakes could stay the same forever. Students are not much different now than they were fifteen years ago."

He nodded agreement. "I hate to see the trees dying," he said.

* * *

I am, by trade, a professional Christian, the university chaplain at

Notre Dame. All of us work, if we make use of our graces, at being faithful to the Catholic faith. I do it as a way of supporting myself, and of saving my soul; a visible practitioner of the Protestant ethic. Students, if they choose, look to me or lean on me, as they would a parent figure in a family. They come asking for guidance on the universal problems.

As a priest, I don't think there's an infallible side of the pulpit; at least, not while I'm in it. I am trustworthy as a guide, smart enough to know my limitations, loving and respectful of the Church. I'm not anxious to ruin someone's life with my ignorance. As a celibate, I am limited as a counselor on sexual intimacy. You can't be an expert on Australia, until you've been to Australia; I would have difficulty locating Australia on the map. However, I can tell the difference between a boomerang and a kangaroo. In the bedroom, as in Tiffany's, all that glitters is not really gold. I've gotten that far in Masters and Johnson.

After a summer in New York, everyone on campus looks healthy and beautiful. A freshman girl sits outside my office weeping. She's a little homesick, but too shy to want to talk yet.

By and by a student will come, needing to argue. Catholics have it all wrong, this student will say. Paradise is gained, not lost, with the surrender of innocence. Sometimes, after listening to the gospel according to *Hustler*, I'm tempted to say: "Okay, you've convinced me. Celibacy for me has been a mistake. Where do I go to make up for lost time?" Someday, I'd like to leave the next to the last word to the argumentative atheist, then finish the conversation with a cry of despair: "You've made me see that He doesn't exist! What do I do with the rest of my life?"

How would some kid with a lot of class handle it if you told him his arguments had destroyed a priest's vocation? A responsible priest couldn't play such games with the feelings of a young person searching for values to live by.

Kindness, like grace, is everywhere. My mother died in Maine in 1982; I lost my father in 1945. The death of a mother is a special time, personal as a birthday. Students, understanding pain, wanted to help. Kathy brought brownies to the door and said: "I've noticed after a funeral, everyone is hungry. Eating seems a way of dealing with sadness. That's the way it was with my family."

Mark wrote a note telling of his mother. "She died when I was real little, but I still remember her. Whenever I'm in a play, when I walk onstage, I ask her to pray for me. Whenever I take an exam, I feel that she's very close, wishing me well."

Mike left a carton of Pall Malls in my room. As he left, he said, "My mother always brought food to the house where a neighbor had died. I hoped, for you, cigarettes would do in place of food."

It is comforting to walk in the footsteps of students who have explored the ground before you; sometimes it is merely scary. A young graduate student describes in chilling detail an early attempt at suicide.

"I knew for years I was going to try it," she said. "My death wish was incredibly strong. That's over with now. I will not try it again."

She said she was quite happy the morning she decided to take her life. For years, she'd been collecting "jelly beans," as she called the pills she had been getting at the infirmary; she had over five hundred of them stashed away.

She went to a quiet place in the woods. She brought

her books, and a blanket to cover herself. If anyone saw her, she reasoned, he would think she was a tired student taking a nap.

She took the "jelly beans" slowly, a couple at a time, so she wouldn't get sick and vomit. She swallowed them with pop to make them easy on the stomach. She stretched out on the ground, and for a long time she didn't feel a thing. A man came along and noticed her. He thought something was funny.

"At the hospital," she said, "my heart stopped three times. I felt really angry when they finally woke me up."

On another occasion a young woman came to me with scars to be healed after a sexual attack. "He brutalized me," she said, "at the point of a knife. Later, at the police station, they said: 'We noticed there are no cut marks on your clothing. Does this mean you undressed voluntarily?'

"I answered: 'Voluntarily . . . at the point of a knife.' I felt they were asking me if I was a tramp."

She looked at me with tears on her face. "I've felt dirty ever since."

* * *

A Frisbee skimmed past my car like an impertinent bird. "Great Scott," I thought, "I'm being attacked by urchins." It turned out to be Michael, getting my attention.

"Watcha thinking about?" he asked. "From your expression, you could be suffering the heartbreak of psoriasis."

"Requiems for a heavyweight," I said. "Pavanes for a dead princess."

"Such a fantastic day of Indian summer," he said. "The trees are giving a gypsy party. You decided to come as a wet blanket."

10

As a faith figure, I get called on to be the morale officer.

"Hey, Mike," I said, "do you want to ask me questions about the existence of God?"

"Not especially," he said.

"Got any hangups you need advice on?"

"You'd better be wearing the purple ribbon around your neck to be asking questions like that. How'd you like to throw a Frisbee?"

"A toy," I sniffed. "Other kids your age are off saving whales."

"The children work, while the old men play," he replied. "How's your golf game coming?"

I decided then and there to give Michael the fifth chapter of the Epistle to the Hebrews — "Every high priest is taken from among men and made their representative before God, . . . He is able to deal patiently with erring sinners, for he himself is beset by weakness. . ." (5:1-2) — as his next penance. It could put ideas in his head. The most you can ever do is plant ideas in a kid's mind.

* * *

A freshman comes through the door, searching anxiously through her information sheets to see if I'm anyone necessary to her life as a student.

"I'm the chaplain," I say.

"What does the chaplain do?"

"I have been described as a wet blanket," I say.

"Oh," she says, not quite polite enough or perhaps quick enough to hide her feelings that I was a waste of time. "Well, I'll come back real soon."

Eventually, I suppose, she will recognize me as the companion to a cocker spaniel, Darby O'Gill II, the only legitimate dog on campus.

There used to be a philosopher at Notre Dame who loved the trees for their quiddities and essences. He would teach the freshmen the difference between the "thisness" of one and the "thatness" of another, until they all understood the pleasing, infinite varieties of sameness. The philosopher gave those students insights they could use to be nature poets; next to being a saint, being a poet is best. Now the philosopher is gone, some of the trees are gone, but there are always freshmen asking the same impertinent questions. I never know how to tell them what I do. "A chaplain spins not, neither does he toil." Definitions don't exist to describe the quiddities and essences of a chaplain.

You hope they will find out anyway. You're the wet blanket until a bad midnight comes along. Then, if you're lucky, a grieving youngster will notice that a wet blanket serves well as a comforter.

Can We Talk?

Can we talk? We are veterans of life, you and I, acquainted with the murkiness called the mystery of iniquity, and not unfamiliar with the victories of grace called moral miracles. Can we talk? Some take the high road leading to an uncritical fundamentalism that causes more faith problems than it ever answered. Others take the low road of skepticism that brings them, naked to their enemies, into the desert places of the heart where there are no hiding places. If you are with me, you go along the median strip, down the pathway of trust, full of detours and potholes that represent discouragement and disappointment. We get lost once in a while in a world that grows shabby; it's like a cheap one-night hotel on the road to Jericho where the Good Samaritan is the guest-master.

I don't write for Christians who are already saved. On the other hand, I have a problem believing that anyone gets lost. The grace of Christ is here. It is busy configuring the souls of sinners who wouldn't recognize the Lord's name as the essential name they should call on if they wish a room in their Father's house. The sunshine makes the flowers grow, and it warms the farmer, his wife, and his children whether they ever think of the sun or not. Jesus, the only begotten Son, is the sunshine and the rain no man can hide from. Born-again Christians may stand proud and tall, like sunflowers, as though they had a monopoly on the light; but violets grow as wild flowers in humble patches near the dump: weeds more chaste than the chrysanthemums that have their price in the florist's shop.

I am one of those Christians who have a lover's quarrel with the world. I believe the Lord had a lover's quarrel with His world. The world can hurt you, and it can kill you, because the world never promised to love you back, since it hasn't the heart for it. How can I say I love heaven, which I have not seen, if I despise the earth lying all around me, regarding it like a slum? The Lord must have loved cities, or He wouldn't have wept over Jerusalem, where He used to go to watch the crowds. He has never minded my loving New York, because He goes there himself. I've seen Him a thousand times in the people that walk with me on the sidewalk.

*   *   *

A student I met late in the evening of Good Friday came back to my room. "Can we talk?" he asked. I was tired, and hoped we wouldn't argue, but I couldn't send him away. He had decided, he said, to deny the existence

13

of evil. What we call evil is just the way things are, he said — meaning, I think, everything has its imperfections and flaws. Eyesight wears out. Hearing fails. Cells go on a reproductive orgy. The mind entertains itself with murderous thoughts. That's the way the cookie crumbles. Evil, if it does not exist, needs no father, like Lucifer or Satan, to beget it.

"In regard to the existence of fallen archangels that have turned into tempters," I said, "I am an agnostic, because I don't read the Bible that literally. The existence of evil seems undeniable. The question is whether evil is mindless, or whether evil is self-concious, knowing its own darkness and conspiring with negation, building an empire for undoing creation."

"Have you read John Steinbeck's *The Grapes of Wrath*?" he asked.

I nodded, saying, "You're thinking of Casey, the transcendentalist preacher: there ain't no good or evil, only things that people do. Some things are nice, and some things hurt; the only real harm is meanness. But it's all part of one big thing; and we're parts of the same thing. And all the parts together add up to the soul in everything, which is a part of God, who wants to keep all the parts fitting together."

He upstaged me by tracing the notion of the Oversoul from Plato to Emerson, with a clever footnote or two from Leibnitz. The University of Notre Dame is going to suffer losses if we keep educating the students to be smarter than the priests.

I said: "I keep hearing the scratching of the mice's feet behind the wall." He looked puzzled, as though he thought I was referring to a pest problem that could be solved by a cat.

"I mean, the wall of the universe," I said. "The Evil

gives itself — himself — away." I could see him flinching at the personal pronoun, which betrayed my anthropomorphic thinking.

He said: "What do you mean?"

"If you hear the notes being tinkled on a piano," I said, "randomly, without order, lacking a tune, you can guess that the kittens are dancing on the keys. But if you can make out a pattern to the sound, with a motif that repeats itself so that you can guess what's coming, you know that experienced hands are at work, showing off their training."

"So," he said, none too respectfully, "the mice's feet heard behind the wall have now gotten into the piano."

"I hope not," I replied, because I don't own a piano. "I keep getting hints of mischief on the loose. I could be misled, as when the branches of a tree brush against the house and it sounds like mice. You can never be sure with a hint."

"By hints, I suppose you mean war and the rumors of war; man's inhumanity to man, and the starving people of Asia?"

"I grew up with war and the rumors of war," I said. "I'm no longer very sensitive to that kind of horror. This seems like a new attack, as if It — He — felt it was time to push His — Its — luck."

"Why would He or It or They give you a hint?"

"I can't prove anything," I said. "I hear something on the news. It makes me sick to my stomach. The news event is so gross that you recognize a deliberate step in an unfolding plan of metaphysical mischief. You have no proof. You wonder if anyone else caught the hint — the threat — attached to the grossness."

I was making him nervous. This was turning out to be more than an amusing game he was playing with a

15

priest, matching his philosophy course against a seminary education over thirty years old. He was dealing with a nut who sprinkled demons with holy water.

"What did you hear on the news that upset you?" he said condescendingly. "Was it about communism spreading?"

"It's the attack on children," I said. "I've heard dozens of stories of outrages committed against children. Something — or someone — in the world hates children, and has declared war."

He said: "Ivan Karamazov turned in his passport of faith in a God who permits the suffering of children. He had collected newspaper accounts of children being killed or abused. Camus' doctor, in *The Plague*, gave up on God because He allowed the painful sickness of children. For two great writers, He was responsible for His universe, and they didn't have to blame the devil as a scapegoat."

I said: "Alyosha, Ivan's brother, who lived in a monastery, pointed out that Christ also suffered like a sinless child terrified by pain. Human suffering is not explained by God's suffering, but at least He is acquainted with it. The forgiveness of sins was brought back from that bleak torture of innocence. Scripture says it was Satan's hour. Now he seems on the move again."

"What's happening that makes you think the children have the cards stacked against them?"

"Abortion, to begin with," I said. "Child abuse, child pornography, molestation, the razor blades in Halloween apples, the rotten Easter eggs that make children sick, drugs on the school playground. . . ."

"It's hardly the Holocaust," he said blandly.

"The Jews in Germany must have gotten their hints the first time they saw an anti-Semitic slogan painted on a church wall. Jews are old hands at reading the handwriting on the wall. But that was another country, where I didn't live with the hatred."

"You shouldn't exaggerate the importance of the garbage that's happening," he said.

"The Jews have often been told they exaggerate the importance of an insult. What has begun as a verbal insult has ended with the cyanide showers of a death camp. I'm not imagining the attacks on children. Is it crazy to want to save them before further harm is done?"

"Save them from what?"

"The final assault on the last great stronghold of human goodness," I said passionately, "which, for all I know, is the final corruption left, before the last judgment of the world. When I read about the thousands of young people ruined by drugs, and the thousands of families torn apart by divorce, I get terrified at the chaos we have consented to. It feels as if we're onstage for the last scenes of a tragedy: the good guys have died, and the children have been sentenced to death. The prince of hell stands grinning at the body count."

"You already admitted you're not sure of the existence of fallen archangels."

"He makes a liar out of me with his proofs to the contrary," I replied.

He figured out I was engaging him in a *tour de force*. I was only half having fun with him; the subject was too serious to be funny. I have the instincts of a fundamentalist when I'm challenged by glibness. Good Friday is a bad day to tell a priest you're denying the existence of evil.

Unanswered Candles In October

The clock was striking two in the morning as I walked with my dog Darby O'Gill II across the Notre Dame campus, behind the main building and down the road leading to St. Mary's Lake, for a few quiet minutes at the grotto. The dog disappeared; and as I wondered where he had gotten lost among the shadows around Sacred Heart Church, he came back in the company of a Notre Dame student named Tim. Darby imagines himself a shepherd's dog, rounding up sheep who can't find their own way home.

Tim told me he was on his way back to his dorm after studying with a friend.

"I'm going to the grotto," I said. "Walk along with me."

In a brief time, we were staring into the collected fires of candles lighted in honor of the Mother of God. We knelt side by side in silent prayer. "Let's say the Hail Mary together," I said.

The dog had disappeared again, the domesticated beast in search of wild things. I'm never in a hurry to leave the grotto. Patient waiting comes easily under a night sky filled with stars.

"I haven't been here since I was a freshman," Tim said. "I used to come down every night. It seemed necessary, like attending the home football games. You outgrow the kid stuff, if you're lucky."

He was baiting me, I felt, into asking him questions. "If you're not lucky," I said, "you keep coming back to the games and the grotto until you're eighty?"

"It's part of the religion of the place," he said. "Knute Rockne, Our Lady's coach. Tom Dooley, dying of cancer, remembering the priests down here, in their oversized coats, brushing the snow off the statues. 'Our Father, who art in heaven. Notre Dame 10, Michigan 7.' "

"So what happened that you stopped needing miracles?" I asked.

"I'm still a Catholic going to Mass," he said, "but I outgrew Disneyland. In high school, I played basketball. As team captain, before any big game, I brought a basketball into the chapel and offered it to the Blessed Mother. I prayed that I would please her with my playing. Whether we won or not, I wanted her to smile at me the way she smiled at the little juggler in the legend."

The legend of the juggler belongs to the other Notre Dame, where Quasimodo played defense for the gargoyles.

"As a freshman at Notre Dame," Tim said, "I did the same thing with a chemistry book. After failing a half-dozen quizzes, I finally figured out I was practicing magic."

It sounded to me as though he had been praying to win, but I didn't tell him so. Socrates would have avoided a hemlock cocktail if he had kept his mouth shut.

"Anyway," Tim said, "I decided there was more important stuff I could be doing as a serious Christian."

I was happy to hear he was a serious Christian. "Like what?" I wanted to know. As a Christian myself, I waste too much time on the peripheral things.

"Visiting nursing homes," he said. "Playing basketball with the black kids in South Bend. Helping out as a Big Brother. Tutoring neighborhood kids in math. Spending Saturdays at the children's hospital."

On the lake, the ducks were splashing and quacking as though fish were nibbling at the webs of their feet. The dog, who had come back to us out of breath, cocked his head to listen. Behind the trees above the grotto, I could imagine Our Lady on the dome dressed in moonlight. The cross on the church spire rising above the bell tower pointed at a moving light that could have been a falling star. Even a serious Christian, I thought, might have use for a spot so much at peace with itself.

"You're lucky Darby found you," I said. "You might have gone to bed without saying night prayers."

"Father," he said, his voice suddenly hard, "does any of it ever seem to you like a crock? Do you believe *everything* they tell you?"

"Not yet," I said.

There used to be a book in the library, never freely circulated, that's been missing for years, which satirizes Catholic tradition. Mary, the Mother of Jesus, through some witch's incantation, is transferred through time. She appears in the Notre Dame stadium at a football game. A language scholar, sitting nearby, recognizes the crude Aramaic dialect of the simple, confused woman. He explains Notre Dame and its faith to her, and the woman thinks how uncomfortable life would be as the Mother of God. In 1941, a Jew, Franz Werfel, in fulfillment of a wartime promise, had a book published about the appearances of Our Lady to the little Bernadette. That book, for me, was the beginning of Catholic grace, but I never said I believed everything.

"The last time I came to the grotto," Tim said, "was the night my mother called to tell me that my father had left her. I had lit a candle every night of my freshman year, praying for my parents to stay together."

This was not a major crisis of faith, yet bitterness heard in a young man's voice sounded like a cry for help. How could I explain the unanswered candles?

20

"Tim," I said, "she's not your fairy godmother." I was ready to help him sort through his doubts, but how do you defend a grotto to a student? "Do you want to talk about your father?"

He shook his head no. "I'd better be getting back," he said.

The priest, the student, and the beast climbed the stairs leading to the real world, where the air was not so alive with the ghosts of prayers. I thought of the children returning from the land of Narnia, though for Tim, it would be more like Oz. The dome with its statue came into sight, so brightly lighted that the moon, directly overhead, looked pale by comparison.

"In Disneyland," Tim said, "they do as much for Mickey Mouse."

"That's not fair," I said. "The Frenchmen who founded the place were missionaries, not artists creating miracles in stone for the cathedral at Chartres. Their work hasn't the freshness of Chaucer's hymns to the Virgin, nor the high poetry of St. Bernard addressing the mother of the Church. In a howling wilderness, they did the best they could."

Moonlight makes fools out of young lovers exchanging promises and old priests arguing faith. No pope ever said that an enthusiasm for grottos was necessary for salvation. I felt the folly of my role-playing as the whimsical cleric companioning a whimsical cocker spaniel on his mock-serious hunt for elusive game.

Darby and I said good-night to Tim, as well as good-morning for the day that would begin soon, all of us friends acquainted with the others' limitations. October, I decided, was a good month for me to read *The Song of Bernadette* again. I'm always touched by seeing how rough Bernadette's life was. Her doctors, testing her, held her hand close to the flame of a candle. Was it necessary, I wonder, to risk hurting her, before they could believe her story?

Outside the door of the dorm, Darby was scolding a bush with his barks. The bush had interfered with his tracking down a field mouse, and the critter got away. I wished the field mouse well. Darby wouldn't have hurt it; he just wanted to get close enough to sniff it. Now his pride was hurt.

I stroked the dog's head as a comfort to his disappointment. "Don't worry, mighty hunter," I said. "You'll be on another chase tomorrow."

Taking a final look at the moon (which, many hours before, looked so promising for harvests and hunting), I took Darby O'Gill II inside. From his snores, he might have been dreaming of his future successes as the hound of heaven. I've told everyone, from the beginning, that he is Our Lady's dog.

Brother Lazarus

At Darby's Place, a campus hangout for the hours after midnight, we were telling ghost stories. I had run all my old favorites up the flagpole, including tales of the supernatural: a picture of the Gipper's ghost reading *Sports Illustrated*; the priest tangling with the devil in the form of a large black dog on the shores of St. Mary's Lake at three in the morning; the seminarian in league with darkness from whose fingertips the holy water in the font shrank back like the retiring tide in the Red Sea. In the glow of a dim bulb, I made them turn their backs so that they could hear how disturbing it sounds when a foot is dragged in a shuffling walk like that of Igor, caretaker of the dead, while Darby O'Gill II growled ominously.

After a while I said, "I'm out of stories, unless I were to tell you about Brother Lazarus."

Joe Dolan, an actor, thought it was his turn to hold the stage. He offered to read Edgar Allen Poe's "The Premature Burial," a short story about a man fearful of waking up in his grave.

Paul, Joe's best friend, had been through "The Premature Burial" too many times to be patient with Joe's performance. "That story adds a new horror to death," Paul said. "A premature burial is impossible in an age where they embalm you."

I said: "My godfather knew of a premature burial years ago, at a time when coffins had glass covers. A widower kept having dreams that his wife had come to life in the grave. He got a court order to dig up the body. The woman, awakening in the darkness, had smashed the glass. The body was bloody from the broken shards."

Joe Dolan said: "The high-school religion teacher told us about the premature burial of Thomas à Kempis, a Dutch priest who wrote the *Imitation of Christ*. He pulled out his hair by the roots and tore the flesh off his face with his fingernails. Finding him like that, the nun told us, they could never canonize him, because he may have died in despair while suffocating."

Christina gave a shudder at how morbid we had become. "I hope you gentlemen are planning to walk me back to my dorm, after frightening me to death."

Joe Dolan, who enjoys scaring girls so that they will cling to him in fear, said he had planned to take her home later.

Christina asked: "Could I get to sleep if I heard about Brother Lazarus?"

"Brother Lazarus is still around," I said. "He could be embarrassed if he is publicized."

"If you tease us with stories you refuse to tell, I shall do something untypical, like studying Greek right here at Darby's," Christina said.

Joe Dolan and Paul swore that they would study Greek with Christina if they couldn't hear the Lazarus story. Those young people were certainly members of the "Now Generation." What else could I do, since they were twisting my arm?

"The brother I am speaking of is called Lazarus behind his back," I began. "He has another name in religion, which I will not mention. For the sake of convenience, I will call him Brother Kevin. I first heard his legend many years ago. The storyteller was a priest entertaining us at a witches' sabbath celebrating *Walpurgisnacht* on the eve of May Day. He wanted us to believe the Lazarus legend was more than superstitious gossip. His grandmother knew a witch who claimed she had danced a jig with Beelzebub on a mountaintop in Germany every April thirtieth since the eighth century. He wished to neutralize his account of the high jinks of the damned with the accredited account of a holy man like Brother Lazarus, so the devil couldn't claim he got the last word. If the priest was spinning a yarn, he never admitted it until the day he died."

Christina shivered as though she was experiencing fear that she found delicious.

I continued:

Once long ago, an Irish lad from Galway found his way to the Midwest where, after working for a while, he applied to enter our community as a novice. In Ireland, he had been a farmer. So,

24

after he made his vows, he was put to work tending the great gardens and caring for the fruit trees the brothers were famous for. He was a good-hearted fellow, loud and boisterous at recreation, but attentive to his prayers, and a great one for spending time on his knees in the chapel. One day a letter arrived from his sister in the city of Galway saying that their father was very sick, and it would be a mercy to the old man if he could see his boy before he passed away. Kevin, with the superior's blessing, took the train to New York, where he caught the boat home.

Kevin wrote when he got to Galway, saying his father was still alive, though he was close to the end. After that, nothing more was heard. The superior kept writing to Kevin's sister's address to find out what was happening. Finally, a letter came from a parish priest saying he had anointed Kevin for death, and buried him with his family in the graveyard of the parish church. The requiems were said for a deceased brother, and he was prayed for by name on the anniversary of his death. His friends said it was sad, God help us, when a young man is swept off unexpectedly, but Kevin would be happy in heaven talking to the saints.

Five years went by. One afternoon, a man who looked familiar — the young Irish farmer in a worn edition — knocked like a stranger on the superior's door. The man identified himself as Kevin, who had been listed so long among the Holy Cross dead. He didn't explain much. His father had died, and then his sister got sick, and Kevin took care of her until she too died. He had gotten sick himself, and spent all his money paying for hospitals. As soon as he was able, he had taken a job to earn the money for his passage to America.

He should have written for help, the superior said. Kevin shrugged in the way the Irish do when expressing their stubbornness. "Our brother who was dead has come back to life," the superior said, and he asked the priests to say a Mass celebrating this miracle of resurrection.

The Kevin who came back was much quieter than the brother who had left. He kept the schedule of the house, spending most of his personal time in the chapel. He was gracious when spoken to, but he barely ever talked. He made the merest pretense of eating, and the brother who was his neighbor claimed he knew for a fact that Kevin never closed his eyes in sleep. He quickly got a reputation as a holy man. When the other Religious expressed their concern over his subdued lifestyle, the superior said: "We have few enough saints, so let's not bother him."

Kevin went back to his work on the farm. One day, when he was plowing a field, he had an accident. The tractor overturned and he was thrown to the ground, where he lay stunned. He was taken to the house, and the doctor was called to examine him for injury. "No bones were broken," the doctor said, "but look at this."

In its undressed state, you could see that the body was mottled with spots like the places on cheese where mold grows. You could imagine that dark decay had started to work on the flesh, and then given up its mindless labor, because time ran out on a hunger that needs the darkness. You could borrow imagery from the Gothic to describe the effects of worms and putrefaction claiming the body that had been called back, as though those horrors could be domesticated and subjected to orders. As the doctor expressed it, the human sack of skin and bones looked like a cadaver that had served time in a hole in the ground. Wounds that had been as soft as jelly, sealed with healing that used the method of annealed glass, left telltale marks, like an "x" standing for the signature of illiterate death. Yet the body looked peaceful, as a battlefield looks peaceful when the war is won. It smelled clean and sweet like a soldier who has bathed after battle, on the way to see his girl.

That was when Brother Lazarus became for his brothers a living miracle who heard a voice that awakened him, as the son of the widow of Naim was awakened. Kevin, from that day, was Brother Lazarus to us.

"Where is he now?" the students wanted to know.

"I was afraid you'd ask," I said. "He's an old man, very fragile. He keeps asking to go back to Galway where Jesus will be waiting for him on a hill by the Irish sea, he says, though he may be daydreaming. He has some business to finish with his mother. The mother he speaks of could be the consecrated ground of his country."

"Will they send him back?" Chris asked.

"He couldn't go by himself," I replied. "The superior could take him, but he's so delicate, he could break apart on the way. They've promised to bury him in Ireland, if he wishes, though the community cemetery is here. Any-

27

way, a number of brothers don't put any stock in Brother Lazarus. They feel he's a holy old gentleman, a bit soft now, whom we've spun fantasies around.''

"Why, if he died, would Christ call him back?" asked Paul.

"Miracles are a sign from God, if you have the grace to believe in them," I said. "If you don't have the grace, resurrections and mysteries are non-events. The community is very proud of Brother Lazarus. He could have been a Jesuit.''

Joe Dolan, skeptical as an Irishman of things he loves the most, looked me straight in the eye. "Have you been handing us a crock?" he demanded.

"Would I lie to the children who made a folk hero out of Luke Skywalker, and had tears running down their cheeks when E.T. went home?"

Christina got out of her chair with the determination of a woman who has suddenly decided to study Greek. She didn't believe me when I told her how the leprechauns got to Ireland. She believes in leprechauns because she's spotted them in the peat bogs smoking their pipes. She hated hearing they were deported from heaven as cowards, hiding from battle during the great war of the angels. Superstition means putting your faith in leprechauns while doubting the experience of Lazarus risen from the dead. It is ignorance she'll be held accountable for in the judgment, when Brother Lazarus as an early riser is getting stars for his crown.

The Celtic Credential

The last conversation I had with Mike lasted three hours because he was a graduating senior who has taken

28

a job at the other end of the earth. Halfway through the evening I went into the chapel to say Mass, and Mike came with me to take it all in, though he isn't a Catholic. I hoped he could feel I was making a personal statement to him by letting him see me as the celebrant so that the liturgy counted for him as part of our talk. Whatever we said that night was good, but it was also sad because it was a final time and we had waited too long to say everything that was on our minds.

He had met this lovely young woman, Catholic and Irish, whom he wanted to marry. His mother said: "Oh, Mike, why must you keep meeting these Catholic girls instead of one of your own kind?" as though his mother felt personally defeated as a Methodist. Mike's father was an Irish Catholic, and now his parents were separated. Legend has it that God promised to deliver the Irish people into the hands of St. Patrick on the day of judgment. Neither Mike nor his mother would have known of the legend, but it might have explained why the poor woman felt she was fighting a battle in which the odds were against her: Celtic confessors of the ancient faith were at work in heaven with their prayers, because they wanted Michael safe in the fold.

Mike said: "My father's downfall was drinking. My mother put up with the drinking as long as she could. Ten years ago, she left him. They've never been divorced. As a Catholic, he wouldn't let her get a divorce. My mother says: 'I couldn't fight his religion. He wears me out with his religion; it means the world to him.' "

I had forgotten that a marriage partner can be jealous of the Church. "The Irish would make life easier for their children if they married other Irish," I said. "My father married an Irish girl. He found it hard to forgive his kids when they let the Irish show."

When Mike talks of becoming a Catholic, I get the feeling of blood's being thicker than water, as though there was a mysticism in being Irish that gets passed on in the genes. He's more of a Catholic than he is a Protestant, yet he hasn't been given the grace to accept his father's religion. His doubts are greater than his faith. He apologized for leaving this unfinished business behind him at Notre Dame.

"I'm disappointed too," I said, too honest to lie.

"I didn't realize that Catholics were different from Protestants," Mike said, "until I went to Mass with my father. I got up to go to Communion, and he put his hand on my shoulder and told me I shouldn't. He was doing something I couldn't do, and I felt very left out."

"He lives his life so that he can stay worthy of going to Communion," I said, guessing. "He has a struggle with drinking, and his wife leaves him. He becomes a stranger to his family and stays alone like a celibate. He doesn't give up his religion or the Mass that will help him save his soul. He is a recognizable type, known in every parish, as wonderful as the Hollywood actors with their marriages on the rocks who stayed faithful to the sacraments in the Church as it was a generation ago."

It did Mike good to hear his father praised. He tends to see his father through his mother's eyes, because he knows her sorrows as a wife. He has mixed feelings toward his father, and hasn't forgiven him for the breakup of the home. "I could never talk to my father," Mike complained. "He was always so far away." The distance he was talking about was chiefly an emotional distance. His father had left town, never looking back on his family, concerned with sobriety and eternal salvation, not caring whether the rest of them were headed for heaven or not.

Not long ago, when Mike was traveling from Notre Dame to London during a campus holiday, I gave him a good-bye hug. He stood there with obvious tears in his eyes, and I wondered why. "In my whole life," he said, "my father never hugged me." The quality of paternalism certainly suffers when an Irishman is reticent.

I said: "It seems to me there are ordinary doubts that every Catholic has, and there are Irish doubts passed down from father to son, from mother to daughter, as a birthright. Ireland, on good days, is holy and emerald-green. On bad days, it is green and it rains incessantly. The chill that gets into the marrow is depressing. I spent a wet week in Dublin once. You couldn't be that miserable for so long a time without feeling God-forsaken. That's when the drinking begins; or, if you're a woman, you compensate with faith, which believes the impossible, mingled with doubt, which is cold-blooded fatalism. Women have always been the great apostles of Irish faith, which they hand on with clear-eyed realism to their sons who become priests. My best friend was an Irish priest who had doubts so well-developed you could have written them down as a catechism for skeptics."

I could have traced the figure of the Irish priest having doubts through fiction and drama; but Mike, wondering why I was spinning my wheels, looked as though he wanted to escape. It was time to move from my antiphon to the text of my lesson. I began:

> My mother, from a family with roots in Galway, married into a Yankee family where the Irish were made fun of as "harps." My father, adoring her, ignored her ancestry (as far as I could see), and my mother mentioned it only to us children. In private, she never let us forget we were

part Irish, but she said we could never be Catholics. You have to be born a Catholic, she said, but once a Catholic, always a Catholic.

Though it was forbidden and impossible, I became a Catholic when I finished high school, never daring to tell my family. I was a kid who became confused by the religion that had me sneaking to Mass, behaving in church like a car thief hiding from the cops. Finally, desperate for a Catholic connection, I went to Boston to see my Irish grandmother, an elderly Catholic woman I had never met. The first time I saw her was in April 1945, during Eastertide, I remember, because I was able to go to Communion openly and make my Easter duty. The second time was the following Christmas, a week after my father died.

I came home from Boston on a Sunday night. I waited until Monday, when my father was at work, to tell my mother I had gone to my grandmother's house. Here was shocking news, for nobody in our house had laid eyes on my grandmother in over twenty years. My mother was sick in bed that day. Her heart was giving her trouble, and I wanted to be very tender. I got the feeling I was opening a door for her that she had closed on the past. She wanted all the news of her mother and her brother and his wife and family.

To my surprise, she asked if I was a Catholic, as though she could smell it like incense on my clothes. I told her I had been baptized a Catholic the previous November, and had the dream of becoming a priest. For months, she had fought me bitterly for talking to the Jesuits who taught in the Catholic high school. Now she said: "I will help

32

you all I can. I don't know what your father will say." She was on my side, acknowledging something dear to her and important to her. For the first time I felt clean as a Catholic. I could go to Mass without breaking my mother's heart. She would keep the Yankees from disowning me. Ten years later, after I was ordained, she became a Catholic herself.

Mike said politely: "That's an interesting story." I told it well so that it would be full of surprises tugging at his emotions. I asked him about the Catholic girl he met. Her name was Mary, he said, and he was crazy about her. He felt like becoming a Catholic for Mary's sake so that their wedding would be perfect. But he couldn't recite a creed he didn't believe, or tell a lie about his relationship to God. He didn't want his marriage to end as a disaster.

So that he would know what was expected of him as the husband of a Catholic, I read him the "Exhortation Before Marriage" from the old *Ritual*: "Sacrifice is usually difficult and irksome. Only love can make it easy, and perfect love can make it a joy. We are willing to give in proportion as we love. And when love is perfect, the sacrifice is complete. God so loved the world that He gave His only begotten Son. . . ." If God's love unites with human love in Christian marriage, Mike and Mary's home will be as holy as a church.

Envisioning the rosy future, I said: "Mike, someday you and Mary, as parents, will go with your young family to Mass, and your father will join you. At Communion, Mary and the children, taking your father's hands, will walk down the aisle to receive. You, as an outsider, will wait for them in the pew. Later, on the way home, your father will ask: 'Mike, when are you going to join us in going to the altar?' With him encouraging you, you'll be ready to see a priest."

"Do you think he will care if I join the Church?" Mike asked wistfully.

"He owes you a faith, legitimizing the Celtic credential that matches the restless Irish blood," I said, for I speak the blarney as well as the Kennedys do.

It would be a while, he said, before he got back to Notre Dame for a visit.

"Life is like a dance," I said pretentiously. "We keep moving past our friends in the opposite direction. We look forward to seeing them the next time around." I gave him my blessing, and we said an affectionate goodbye that left dampness on my cheeks. I wondered if it would be a mistake to call his father to put a bug in his ear. I asked myself: If I did call his father, would his mother, whom I feel sorry for, forgive me? She got caught in a Gaelic game of gain and loss. The dice are loaded in favor of the house. I am a member of an older generation, seeing for itself that the games of grace are rigged, and the odds of winning are in favor of the house.

CHAPTER 3

Shadows Of A Child

I have a weekly radio program called "The Children's Hour," mainly devoted to storytelling. Most of my listeners are probably adults, which I have never minded, especially when the weather is good. The children should be having fun outdoors. During graduation weekend, our story was Saint-Exupéry's *The Little Prince*. The Little Prince came from a tiny planet with a single rose, one sheep, and three volcanoes (one of them extinct so that its young ruler used it as a footstool).

The Little Prince makes his exit from home with a flock of migrating birds, as though birds become space travelers when the seasons change. After much hopping among planets as small as his own, he finally lands in the middle of the African desert, where he meets the aviator Tony, whose plane has crashed on the sands. Soon, the aviator needs to comfort the homesick boy, who is afraid his sheep will eat his flower. The Little Prince, Tony finds, is a perceptive child who sees through the absurdities of adults preoccupied with "matters of consequence."

He is befriended by a fox who teaches him the ritual of taming a wild creature. The fox tells him: Whatever you tame, as you have tamed your flower, becomes uniquely yours. Whatever is essential is invisible, seen only by the heart.

Now a year has passed since the Little Prince left his volcanoes unattended. His planet stands above the desert in the night sky, too small to see among the stars, and he wants to go home while conditions are favorable. A snake, yellow and thin like a gold bracelet, offers him a powerful poison to help him make the journey, as his body is too heavy to take along and will have to be left behind.

Tony is horrified at the sight of the snake and at the thought of the Little Prince being harmed by the snake. The boy assures him it is the only way. His shell will be left in the desert, he says, but there is nothing fearful about a shell. He comforts the aviator with his lovely promise: At night, on my planet, I will laugh for you. When you open the window at night, you will hear the stars laughing.

The yellow snake makes its quick visitation. By daybreak, the small body has disappeared. For seven years, the aviator has kept green his sorrow at the Little Prince's leaving. The laughter he hears from five hundred million stars is like the ringing of bells.

Who is the Little Prince, and what does he represent, and what is the symbolism of the snake — that creature so cursed in our religious tradition? Such answers are mostly personal. It looks to me as though the aviator, fearfully alone after a desert plane crash, suffering from thirst, has this reverie in which he finds the boy he once was, who got left behind in the lost childhood. Literature is the place the lost children are kept at endless play, as timeless as Grecian urns. Remember the poem "To Any Reader" concluding *A Child's Garden of Verses?*

As from the house your mother sees
You playing round the garden trees,
So you may see, if you will look
Through the windows of this book,
Another child, far, far away
And in another garden, play.
But do not think you can at all
By knocking on the window, call
That child to hear you. He intent
Is all on his play-business bent.
He does not hear; he will not look,
Nor yet be lured out of this book
For, long ago, the truth to say,
He has grown up and gone away,
And it is but a child of air
That lingers in the garden there.

On the air with the Little Prince, I wasn't the least mindful of my own lost childhood, because I know where those bones lie a-bleaching, in the Hundred Acre Wood, near Pooh-bear dressed up as a cowboy. In the backwash of graduation, I felt downright tearful over the lost tykes I will never see again. "Is this the little girl I carried? Is this the little boy at play?" sang Tevye and Golda, in a sunrise-sunset mood at their daughter's wedding. Bachelors too have feelings that are tender. I have met wonderful little citizens, housebroken and domesticated, completely perfect as moppets and urchins; beautiful to see; an adventure to talk with; playmates worth cultivating; and so I let them steal my heart. I wrap my happiness into their happiness, their well-being into my well-being. In every way I can think of, I make an investment of my enthusiasm, being careful to remember I don't have a parent's right to spoil them or make them dependent on me.

Then, because of necessary duties, I turn my back for the twinkling of an eye, and when I look around again, the nine-year-olds are seventeen, about to graduate from high school. I like the seventeen-year-olds, especially if I can see the resemblance that convinces me of the ways the child is father to the man. The rose, unfolding, fulfills the beauty that was promised in the bud — at least, I have to pretend it does.

Even when the ripening graces of soul and body have formed a tentative, transitory conclusion of singular charm — even when Rebecca of Sunnybrook Farm grows up to be the sweetheart of the Grange — still, you can feel sadness that the young radiance shopping for a wedding gown will never again be a moppet in a pinafore, eating popcorn.

This is the lost childhood that is unavailable as a re-run; the amnesia of age leaves only bright scattered images you're not really sure of. The first time it happened, I was surprised at the sharpness of the disappointment. Going away, I left an extraordinary child. Coming back, I met an adolescent. She was very nice, but no one I recognized. The child I had worshiped disappeared, and it didn't even feel as though she had left a replacement.

Childhood goes quickly. There is no need to push children to be wise beyond their years. I hate to read newspaper letters signed "by Samantha, age ten," in protest of nuclear war. Children, encouraged by adults to be prophetic, merely sound shrill. The most sickening of all failures are children's crusades, because children, carrying banners, get exploited. Children are never more beautiful, I think, than when they are childlike.

I have a good time with children. I don't mind their wisecracks, slapstick, or stand-up comedy. I'm good-natured when they make remarks about my smoking, until they try to hide the cigarettes. I get uncomfortable if they tell me jokes as sexually explicit as at the local gay bar. It's not my business to tell parents how to raise their families, even if they ask me. I haven't the grace of state to be a parent.

I knew a woman in New York who had two sons. She watched them as protectively as a hawk. When they were outside, she was outside with them. When they went to school, she got a job in the cafeteria so that she could walk them back and forth and be around all day. She bought them bicycles to ride on the sidewalk, making them promise to stay away from the traffic. They were nice children, liked by everyone. They understood their mother's protectiveness. Hell's Kitchen is hard on kids. A lot of children don't make it, dying young from drugs.

One night a drunken driver came speeding up Tenth Avenue and lost control of the car. The wheels jumped the curb, and the car bounded along for half a block. One of the boys, on his bicycle, got hit and was killed instantly. His mother was an eyewitness of the accident. The police said later the driver was so drunk he couldn't remember where he had stolen the car. If I were a parent, I'd be tempted to build a wall to keep harm out.

Children living in the concrete jungle never meet foxes asking to be tamed. The flowers that become unique for them live in a window box. Childhood is when they are in greatest danger, because they can't defend themselves, and their parents are happy to see them get street-wise. Any stranger they meet could be the snake offering poison for the journey to kingdom come. Literature has lots of nice stories with the theme of the lost childhood. In Times Square, they can tell you stories of kids who never had a childhood at all.

I saw *E.T.: The Extra-terrestrial* in a theater on Times Square. I left the movie walking behind a black mother with her four- or five-year-old. At the door going outside, the little girl turned. Lifting her hand, she folded and unfolded her fingers in a wave to the screen. "Goodbye, E.T.," she called, "good-bye."

Astronomers estimate that there are two hundred billion *billion* stars in the universe. (Two hundred billion billion is the same as two hundred quintillion, or "2" followed by twenty zeros.) E.T. went home to one of these stars. Now the night sky is different for children who see essential things, visible to the heart. The extraterrestrial has become their garden of verses. From their ghetto windows they can hear the stars laughing. I don't hear them, but it doesn't matter. The singing, like Christmas, is mostly for children.

A Private Pentecost

If I were to imagine God as discouraged or tired or showing His years — which are a considerable number when you remember that He is older than the everlasting hills — I would know I was wrong, from looking at the freshness of children.

God is beyond everything we can imagine. There is nothing or no one we can compare Him with; but in our human way of speaking, we're tempted sometimes to credit Him with the blues, as when He says of himself in

Green Pastures: "Even being de Lawd ain't no bed of roses." From Cain's murder to the latest outrage against the soldier's widow, God knows the pain. Yet the Holy Spirit keeps tirelessly and good-naturedly busy, giving us the beauty of a sacramental universe; sunsets and evening stars, and shy violets on their mossy banks. Lovelier than anything else in nature is the fresh beauty of children's faces, evidence of how young God thinks after endless ages.

For the sake of children, a covenant of caring is established. Every marriage has in it something of the lawgiving at Sinai and the sacrificial loving with which the Lord opened His heart to the heart of the world in the fellowship of a meal in an upper room. Even without testaments, children are a promise of love that God has kept. Astronomers examine the heavens for signs of cosmic caring; Christmases, when you think of it, were never as distant as that.

Once, I was very close to three children: Laura, Billy, and Chris. Laura, at eleven, was the oldest. On the verge of becoming a woman, she needed assurance she was going to make it gracefully. Billy, at nine, was a problem child; as a living hellion, he was certifiable as a lawbreaker, having been summoned to the police station for a talk with the sergeant after setting off fire alarms and cutting down trees in the Boston Garden. Chris, at six, was a little princess. She needed to be told twenty times a day that she was a little princess, and promised a diadem a princess could wear.

In the absence of their father, I undertook to help the family. The children had known a lot of pain in their lives; they didn't need more pain from me. They allowed me to love them, and be patient and gentle; but anger was always a mistake. Anger made me like everyone else in an adult world, which was already angry with them for daring to be born. They couldn't deal with me as a bad-tempered grown-up, yelling corrections. They detached themselves from caring as my temper rose; their detachment was a defense against feeling hurt that I had turned against them.

Billy, above all, would put me to the test, to see if I really cared. He was an elf-child in appearance and behavior; you would think the devil had tainted his mother's milk, from all the mischief that was in him. He must have grown up feeling as though a malignant star had shone on his birth, because he had been physically abused from infancy. He wanted acceptance: yet if you offered it, he would break your heart to prove whether you meant it.

The only rules I knew were attentiveness and patience. Laura would swear to you that she was the plainest child in New England; her legs were too long, and her neck was too long, and eventually, she believed, her eyes would shrink to the size of raisins from the strain of reading. I praised her legs as a dancer's, and asked if she had considered ballet. I brought her jewelry so that she would like her throat, and ribbons that would look well in her hair. I sent her to an oculist, to get fitted for contacts. I offered her invitations: "How proud I would be, if you and your friend would join me for lunch."

Seated in a restaurant, I would say: "See how the young men are watching us? The older men are probably making plans to take their daughters for a meal." Words that gave pleasure represented my best efforts to light up smiles in the bleakest corners of her face. I tried to help Laura the way a father would help. I did as much as I could.

Antoine de Saint-Exupéry, as mentioned earlier, has a lovely chapter on taming a fox. I'm not sure if I tamed Billy, or he tamed me. After two years of seeing him as unreasonable as chaos, I taught him to trust me. Love, says the Apostle Paul, is patient; with Billy, I learned patience, beginning with the primer. Love, for Billy, was not a now-I-give-it, now-I-take-it-away thing. You didn't have to earn it, you didn't have to deserve it, if it was love. If love was sincere, it would hang around long after you might have thought you had worn it out. You might be desperate for love, but you would give no one your heart for the asking. It had to be won.

He offered me sulks, rejections, temper tantrums, and indifference. I found it was foolish to bribe a child with gifts, or to let him manipulate you, to get his own way. In fairness, all Billy wanted was for me to accept him as the devil's brat he really thought he was. He expected me to hold on, even while he tried to break away, or drive me away with his impishness. He fought to be a loner, hating to be a loner. Finally, he loved me for sticking around as his friend. I think I turned the boy's life around for him. I might not have been the best one to do it, but there was nobody else even trying.

Hard-nosed at nine from being bounced around a lot, he was still just a kid, capable of whimsey, at home in Disneyland, young enough to be patient with Winnie-the-Pooh and the cast of animals from *The Wind in the Willows*.

He said cute things which made the nuns think he would grow up to be a priest. He told one of them he liked going to Communion. She asked him why. "Well," he said, "it's the kind of bread: when you eat it, and you're hungry, after you eat it, you're not hungry any more."

"Wouldn't it make you shiver?" the nun said. I told

her of flowers he had pulled up in the Common, and of birds he had hurt throwing rocks, because of a row he had with his grandmother who lushes.

"Children," the nun said, "have such a strong sense of justice. It makes them hard on adults who hurt them. In their innocence, they never need mercy, or dream of offering it. Later on, Billy will be more forgiving of his grandmother."

"I just want him to be happy," I said. "I want the three of them to be happy."

As for Chris, Billy's junior sibling, she needed to be given an identity, and to be cherished as a person. A little girl's ego can be as needful of attention as a bishop's. She can't be left alone like a baby, having to whine to get attention. Chris knew all the stories of life in the enchanted castle, and she knew she had to be somebody's little princess, if her dreams were to come true.

"What is essential is seen by the heart," wrote Saint-Exupéry. Children, having imaginations, understand this. Sometimes, for grown-ups, a private Pentecost is needed before they are as wise as children, trusting the reasons of the heart. Whenever, in my own life, I want to understand the truth about something, I try explaining it to the children. That is the real reason why, for many years now, I have said a Sunday morning Mass for the urchins. We examine the Catholic faith, trying to find words to say if the mysteries are true, or if the truth is mysterious. If it sounds dumb to them, it will sound dumb to me, and we never lie to one another. I remember the Sunday a youngster heard the choir singing: "Eat My Body, drink My Blood / and we'll sing our song of love."

"Eat My Body, drink My Blood," echoed the child. "Ugh."

The "ugh" was on the side of truth. A badly written song, in its lyrics, had divided the living Person of Christ with grotesque imagery. A theology of the Eucharist should be more carefully stated. An urchin could have told you better. Even the hard-nosed Billy, with his exquisite hunger, could have told you that the Eucharist is not a cannibal's feast.

Children know a language that Berlitz never taught. They are themselves a language, God's word to us on days when He does not use fire.

In them, mankind's springtime, the earth is renewed. Whatever is essential, God lets them see with their hearts.

Cry Uncle

Four children, who pretend I'm their uncle, asked me to tell them a story.

"In the beginning, God created the heavens and the earth," I said. "He had an idea in His mind of what the heavens and the earth should look like. So, *ex nihilo*, beginning from scratch, He put up a firmament, and hung up the moon, the sun, and the stars. He made the world so big that even flights of angels standing on each other's backs couldn't see the edge of it. He set His creation spinning like a top so that there could be night and day and the change of seasons. Finally, on an August morning, when the world was looking like a resort hotel in Miami, He invented Adam and Eve to be His permanent guests in Eden."

"How did God make the world?" asked Timmy, a seven-year-old whose father is an architect making blueprints for buildings. The question meant: how many trucks and bulldozers did His construction company use for hauling and pushing dirt?

Tammy, Timmy's twin, fell into a fit of giggling at the idea of God hassling with day laborers over union contracts. Her opinion, she said, was that God separated the waters from the dry land by magic, as Mary Poppins would have done it. He popped the constellations into place by wrinkling His nose.

"At the end of six days, He would have a tired nose," said Nan, an older sister, "depending on whether He wrinkled separately for every tree and bird, or if He wrinkled once for all the species of birds, and again for all the varieties of trees."

"Six days?" said Bert, who was practically a ninth-grader. "Six billion years would come closer. Charlotte, North Carolina, by itself, took six million years to evolve. Charlotte is just a pup, considering the age of Egypt and the River Nile." Bert wrote letters to a girl from Charlotte, so he kept abreast of the history of the town.

"That's silly talk," said Nan. In Sunday school, she studied God. Evolution is silly talk to people who read their Bible.

Four young faces turned to me, as the troublemaker, for an opinion. I said: "Imagine the Father, the Son, and the Holy Spirit in prayer to themselves, realizing: 'It's not good for Us to be alone,' and God had the idea for the world. God decided to let the idea of the world exist outside His mind, and the idea was the blueprint He used. The idea hovered like a gull in search of water over the abyss of nothingness, until nothingness became something that had a shape like the idea that began in the mind of God. The idea could be compared to the seed that falls in the ground and waits to become a flower. The acorn waits longer to become an oak tree than a bulb waits to turn into a tulip. God lets living things take as much time as they need. He is also patient with mountains being formed out of molehills."

"What did the idea for the world look like?" asked Timmy.

"It looked like more things than you can imagine," I said, "or maybe it was skinny with long legs. What would one of your ideas look like if it existed outside your mind?" You should never let a seven-year-old push your back to the wall.

"Is God magic?" asked Tammy.

"He's not make-believe," I said, on firm theological ground. "Magic is make-believe, and make-believe is always in a hurry. In stories of magic, impromptu tea parties are held on the ceiling. Carousel horses take off on a cross-country steeplechase without a moment's notice, at the whim of a nanny. Miracles are planned an eternity ahead, in conformity with the will of God. God is a miracle-worker, but not a magician."

Bert said: "Maybe God's idea looked like a spark of lightning igniting a gas you couldn't see with your eye."

"Maybe it did," I replied. "I have no idea."

"It seems to me that the boys in this family are always agreed with, even when the boys are wrong," said Nan in anger. "The Bible tells the story of how God created the world. It never mentioned that Eden looked like a hotel in Miami."

"Nor that Adam and Eve had bagels for breakfast," I agreed. "Do you suppose Adam and Eve ate bagels, Nan?"

"Grown-ups shouldn't make fun of the Bible in front of little children," she said.

I apologized for teasing her. "Neither Moses nor the priest-writers who wrote Genesis knew *how* God created the world. They may have thought they knew, but God didn't tell them everything. On the other hand, evolutionists can't tell you *why* the world exists. The Bible tells me of the love which lies behind the Word that shaped creation.''

Timmy had been busy with a crayon, drawing a skinny creature with long legs, and rainbows in its hair. He titled his picture "God." Tammy had gone to her room. Coming back, she announced she had just had a conversation with God. He had told her that, yes, He wrinkled His nose when He made ugly things He didn't like, like mosquitoes and black dogs that frighten kids.

I said she must have misunderstood, because God doesn't have a nose. She said He had to have a nose to wear His glasses on. Finally, I got her to agree that God, if He has a nose, would never use it the way Samantha, the witch on television, uses her nose, because Samantha is magic, and God is miracle. Samantha is make-believe; God is real, and wears glasses.

Timmy explained his drawing by pointing out that God isn't fair, because He never answers prayers, even when you make Him promises. Long legs and skinniness represented a theological opinion.

"Why the rainbow?" I asked.

"Because sometimes He's nice," Timmy said.

Tammy wanted to know if being born was a miracle. "A baby is one of the greatest miracles," I replied.

Timmy asked if dying was a miracle. I said: "If we could see what God sees, we would understand the way death is the gateway to a miracle."

Tammy said: "We had the cat put to sleep." I said that for the cat, perhaps being put to sleep was the gateway to a magic kingdom.

Bert, with his eighth-grade doubts, asked if John

Lennon's death was the gateway to a miracle. "Is death the gateway to a miracle if it comes as an execution by the state?"

"Even a criminal's dying," I said, "is a soul going home to God."

"If he's going to the other place, is it the gateway to a miracle?" Bert insisted.

"The Catholic writer Graham Greene said: 'We know there's a hell. We don't know if anyone has ever gone there,' " I replied.

Bert now felt he had my back to the wall. One of us had to cry uncle, and he was the nephew. The Lord was punishing me for sounding unctuous. The circumstances of our entrances and our exits are holy secrets. You should never say more than you know to a child.

I said: "A sparrow falls out of the winter sky. Heaven is attentive to the death. A season or two ago, instinct handed down in a thousand generations of nests taught the young wings to fly. What happens to the flutter lost from weary wings?"

Their eyes took me seriously as they shook their heads.

"Providence puts it away like a pair of warm mittens. The blood of Christ streams over the firmament. Nothing gets lost forever."

Bert and Nan excused themselves to do homework. Timmy drew a picture of a sparrow wearing mittens on its wing-tips. Tammy asked me to read her a story of a giant wearing a magic pair of glasses.

Guest uncles are a bore when they talk over your head. Children should be taught that truth is bigger than their little minds, I always say; that way, they won't grow up to be bigots.

No Time For Frisbees

In the final chapter of the Pooh stories, Christopher Robin, coming to an end of things, sits, with his chin in his hand, looking out over the world, wishing it wouldn't stop. Finally, he interrupts the summer silence to tell the Bear of Very Little Brain: "I'm not going to do nothing any more."

"Never again?" asks Pooh.

"Well, not so much. They won't let you."

Nothing, Christopher Robin had admitted, was what he liked doing best. When Pooh asks how you did nothing, Christopher Robin explained: It's when people call out at you just as you are going off to do it, what are you going to do, Christopher Robin? And you say, oh, nothing, and then go and do it.

"Oh, I see," said Pooh.

"This is a nothing sort of thing we are doing now."

"Oh, I see," said Pooh again.

"It means just going along, listening to all the things you can't hear, and not bothering."

"Oh!" said Pooh.

Christopher Robin was beginning the responsibilities of his school days. He was leaving an enchanted place in the woods called childhood, where a boy and his stuffed animals play all the day long. There were "ho-hum" things he wouldn't get to do very much, because "they" wouldn't let you. Nobody has ever needed to explain who "they" are. All of us have met them.

Every year, at graduation time, I lay aside Nietzsche and read Chapter 10 of *The House at Pooh Corner*. I recommend it to all the hobbits, facing the end of their fellowship in Middle Earth.

When he was very young, about the age of Christopher Robin, this big-time executive with his company told me that he said good-bye one day to his Velveteen Rabbit and tucked it away in a drawer where his outgrown clothes were kept. He buried certain personal treasures, which he would not be using again, in the backyard. He made a valedictory visit to places in the fields behind his house where he had played every day since he was old enough to be allowed to go off by himself. In his room, he took down some Hummel pictures of babies being watched by guardian angels, which had looked down on his bed from the time he was christened. He cleared the wall, dispassionately disposing of characters from Doctor Seuss and Disney World, and from the Hundred Acre Wood familiar to Eeyore and Kanga, and from the guest list at Toad Hall, known as the elegant ancestral home of the fashionable Mr. Toad by every child who has read *The Wind in the Willows*.

Without sentimentality, he shoved the beloved junk of his early life into a suitcase once used by his grandmother, and hid it away in the back of the closet, where he would see it only if he went looking. Then, closing the door of his room, he turned his back on the past, at least until bedtime. He was ready now, he felt, to face life. Tomorrow, he would be attending his first day of school.

School — said the executive, who was young enough to remember — was no problem for a boy who refused to look back. He hated the feeling of the freshly-ironed shirt he put on clean every morning. He loved reading and writing, and he was the first child in his second grade class to use ink. He never liked paying attention to fractions; geography was a bore when you had to memorize the chief imports of Lithuania instead of daydreaming over the shapes of trees outside the classroom windows. He survived the good days and the gray days as a happy

51

young scholar. If his mother ever noticed that sometimes at night, after there'd been fighting at school, the Velveteen Rabbit had found its way back to a place on his pillow, she never embarrassed him by mentioning it.

* * *

Mike was a senior, clearing out his room and feeling sentimental at leaving. "Is there anything you can use?" he said, pointing at a pile of junk.

I picked up a Frisbee and said, "If I could coach, I would coach Frisbee."

"It's a kid's game," he said. "It has no future as a varsity sport."

"Not as the Irish play it," I said. "There are Third World talents. Put Frisbees in the hands of Latinos in New York. They sail them like birds."

He took the Frisbee and held it up like a priest offering the host. "I bought it in Daytona," he said, "on spring break in my freshman year." Obviously, it represented some formative experience of April in a vintage season, whose lost days he would always speak of as belonging to his best years.

He skimmed it back onto the pile of trash. "There's no time for Frisbees where I'm going to be," he said. One would have thought he was joining the Trappists. The truth is, he hadn't found a job yet.

"Why are you throwing it out?" I said. He looked at me as though he felt old enough to explain to me the facts of life.

"I've applied to the business school at Harvard," he said. "I've taken a job interview with Price Waterhouse. Eventually, I may have to serve a hitch with the Marine Corps. There's a real world out there. They laugh at the guys who keep on using the greasy kid stuff."

"Oh, I see," I said, sounding like Pooh-bear, who, as

a Bear of Very Little Brain, never understood anything.

"Did you ever read the Christopher Robin stories?"

"Probably," he said. "I don't remember."

Metaphors should be made of sterner stuff than the whimsey of A.A. Milne. About a hundred times a week, in talking or preaching, I try to find the accurate images. That's half of what education is all about, trying to find the precise language that hands on experience like an apostolic succession. Who is man, this impudent by-product of evolution, risen like froth to the top of creation's kettle; and having arrived, insisting on his personal immortality that began, he says, with a far-off Eden? Only such stuff as dreams are made of, says Shakespeare. We could have guessed, says Newman, merely by looking, at some long-ago quarrel that distanced man from his origins and destiny. On ordinary days, whimsey seems as true as archetypes: sorrow's story is told in the myth that begins with the dream of the lost childhood.

"Mike," I said, "there *is* life after college."

"I'm betting on it," he said. "Would you like a poster of the Rolling Stones?"

I could have told him of Old Grads who come back for their reunions. They drink a little beer, and swap the old stories. Eventually, some paunch-belly says to some fifty-year-old jogger: "Can we get our hands on a football?" An aging handball player offers to drive them a hundred yards across campus to buy a football. The three of them pile into a limousine to go shopping. They get everything they need for a game with the Dallas Cowboys. By now, it's nearly time for supper. They talk about getting up teams for the morning.

The next day, of course, it is raining. They weren't serious about playing, anyhow. They have gone through a ritual that makes them feel young; such rituals are important to middle-aged men. The new football, in mint condition, rides home in the limo to Perth Amboy, New Jersey, where, as an authentic Notre Dame pigskin, it becomes a conversation piece. Conversations are the tributes we offer our symbols. Every man is less interesting than the symbols he keeps.

* * *

Coventry Patmore has a poem called *The Toys*. The poet has punished with severity his motherless little boy. Later, fearing the child's sorrow will keep him awake, he visits the bedroom where the small son has cried himself to sleep.

> And I, with moan,
> Kissing away his tears, left others of my own;
> For on a table drawn beside his head
> He had put within his reach
> A box of counters and a red-veined stone,
> A piece of glass abraded by the beach.
> And six or seven shells,
> A bottle with bluebells,
> And two French copper coins, ranged there with careful
> art,
> To comfort his sad heart. . . .

We hope for God's compassion, says the poet, touched as He remembers "of what toys / We made our joys," when we sleep in death in His fatherly presence.

* * *

In that enchanted place called Galleons Lap, a little boy and his bear will always be playing. From there, they can see the whole world spread out until it reaches the sky, and whatever there is all the world over is with them in Galleons Lap. Once you leave an enchanted place, and try to go back, nothing again is ever exactly the same.

54

CHAPTER 4

Memories Of A Shorn Lamb

"Do you remember the story Uncle Elmer told?" my sister Barbara asked me. "One Christmas, he was drinking, and he fell asleep under the Christmas tree. He woke up and saw the lights and heard music from the radio. Elmer said he thought he had died and gone to heaven."

"That's an Uncle Elmer story all right," I said, "but I never heard it before." My sister lives in a rest home, because she is not entirely well. She dwells on the past in her mind. She is constantly surprising me with her memories. Some of them are painful to deal with.

"Do you remember Uncle Elmer's dog, Blitzen?" she asked.

"Sure," I said. "Blitzen was the first dog I ever met. He was a Doberman, as gentle as Lassie, with the constantly strong odor of a heated caribou. When they put him to sleep, half the puppies in the neighborhood were left fatherless."

"You were named after Uncle

Elmer," she said. She didn't have to remind me. I've lied about my real middle name for many years.

"Do you remember," she said, "one time asking Daddy what was the good of a belly button? Daddy said it was so that you would have a place to put salt when you ate celery in bed."

I almost can't stand it when my sister remembers stories I had forgotten fifty years ago. My sister doesn't mean to play on my emotions. Every memory she recalls makes her seem a little more tragic. All her life seems to belong to yesterday.

She reaches for her pocketbook. She's going to show me more pictures. She's a walking archive of family history. I have to defend myself against nostalgia.

"Honey," I said, "we'll look at pictures some other time." It was selfish of me. Without her pictures and memories, she has little to talk about.

"I had a little kitten," she said. "Last week, it got run over. The family I live with don't think I should get another one."

"Why not," I asked, "if it would keep you company?"

"I don't have very good luck," she said. "The last one got killed by a dog."

I can never stay by myself with my sister for more than an hour. In her mid-sixties, she's almost totally deaf. The hearing aid we got her drove her crazy. I don't mind repeating — and shouting at her doesn't bother me. She seems, more than anyone I have ever met, the victim of original innocence.

Innocence is a beautiful quality, if you're establishing an identity as a child of God. It can leave you exposed, if you're planning marriage. It can make you fragile, like a glass unicorn. How could we have told Barbara she was too precious for everyday use?

56

My sister, if I asked her, would become a Catholic tomorrow. She would join the Church for my sake. Of the children, she's the most Yankee in outlook. She's a typical Down Easterner in many ways, on uneasy terms with the Catholic religion. For my sake, she would become Catholic, disbelieving more than she ever accepted of sacrament and doctrine.

When one has never lost original innocence, the ordinary rules don't apply. One might wrap a diamond, hard on all its surfaces, in the softness of lamb's wool as a way of protecting the stone; but it wouldn't be necessary. If God is faithful to His promises of gentle dealings with the shorn lamb, the imposition of Catholic creeds would be as superfluous as lamb's wool as a way of putting Barbara's life under the care of heaven.

If faith is needed, I have enough for both of us; she can travel home on a ticket with me. If goodness is essential, I hope to coast to glory on her skirt tail. In our Father's house, where there are many mansions, I'll be lucky if He lets me pay board. Barbara, I expect, will be offering tea to the saints as the hostess of her own condominium.

My mother took care of Barbara for as long as she could. One day, about twenty years ago, after the births of two fine children in a marriage from which a husband has long disappeared, my sister retired into the private life of her mind, where she was at home with her happiest times as a child. For seven years, she needed the protective help of a hospital. When she left the hospital, we knew that from then on she would always be childlike in her ways. She was in no shape to join the rough-and-tumble life of everyday existence.

She would look at you with questions in her eyes, straining to hear, wanting to oblige, fearing you were

57

trying to hurt her. Her loneliness touched me most. To tell the truth, her loneliness has kept me away. I have awakened in the middle of the night to find her sitting, in darkness, on a chair beside my bed.

"What's the matter?" I asked. "Are you feeling sick?"

"I didn't like being by myself," she said. "The quiet made me nervous. Go back to sleep. I won't bother you."

I tried to sleep, holding her by the hand. Finally, because her eyes were a language asking for help, I got up and talked, calming her, until she finally slept in the chair.

She is better now. I can get her laughing, and she makes me laugh again at the old family jokes. Yet I keep running away, because she is so unbearably sad. Old pictures can be an embarrassment. Old stories can leave you as homesick as though you were viewing the earth from the far edges of the moon. It can't be helped. I'm her last link with childhood, and she is mine, the survivors who knew Uncle Elmer and his gamey dog.

Not long ago, in a department store, I saw a lovely child holding a lovely doll, sitting on Santa Claus's lap. The child's mother was watching as the photographer took the little girl's picture. I thought: Barbara must have pictures like that in her pocketbook.

I'm definitely not dreaming of a white Christmas. The great feast of the Church, pointing toward happier celebrations, stretches me apart, as when I talk to a deaf woman living in the heart of memory.

"Remember the plates left on the kitchen table," Barbara asks, "as though Santa had stopped for a lunch? Remember the cigarette in the ashtray, as though he had been smoking?"

I can imagine the look on my father's face as he arranged the evidence of a visitor for his children to find.

Barbara never explained why my namesake uncle positioned himself under the tree like an unwrapped gift. I suspect if it were me and I had been drinking, in a year when I was dreading Christmas, a white one or a dry one, I would have been under the tree waiting to see St. Nicholas. I would have asked him to give me back the magic that only the children really see. I would have asked for the innocence to believe again like a little child.

I wonder if Uncle Elmer was disappointed when he found he was looking at the lights of a tree.

My sister always leaves me with something to think about after her little stories. She makes me a gift of my lost childhood.

On Second Sight

My Irish grandmother, who lived in Boston, never came to our house — partly because she was Irish, but mostly because she was Catholic. I never met her until I was nineteen. She had said hard things to my father on the subject of religion. She was Irish all the way through, and not a hybrid like me. Once, as a girl in Ireland, she had gone to a saint's well to be cured of a sickness. The daughters of St. Patrick keep very faithful after they've had their miracle from a canonized saint.

I first went to see my Irish grandmother in April of 1945, to tell her I wanted to be a priest. She was very old, and we never got well acquainted. On December 15, 1945, my father died. The week after the funeral, I went to Boston to inform the old lady of the death in the family. She felt very bad, though I don't remember anything she said. The next morning, she heard me singing in the bedroom. She came to the door and asked me not to sing, because my father had died. All I remember my Catholic grandmother ever telling me was that a boy who had just lost his father should not be singing — out of respect for the dead. (She died in 1950 when I was a novice and not allowed to go to Boston for the funeral.)

My mother finally went to see my grandmother before she died. My mother stayed away nearly thirty years because of my father, to whom my grandmother had wished bad luck as a punishment. She probably would not have spoken the harsh words if the priest had not gotten after her, my mother thought. A Yankee like my father winces when he's been hit in the head with an Irish grudge. Irish curses have a dark magic to them as though the devil would back them up, and you wish they had never been spoken. Once out, they are on their mischief-making way, and they can't be called back even with prayer. Irish poetry has a sadness that plucks at the heartstrings. You wonder if the history of Ireland would have been better if it had not been doomed by the melancholy of its poets.

My grandmother was too old and gentle to harm a fly. My father must have found her words unkind, even if he did not believe they had the power to change his luck. By the time he died, he grieved just the way she had hoped he would grieve. Perhaps she was enough of an Irish earth mother that intuitions of truth could speak through her.

A student named Christina (mentioned earlier, in Chapter 2), who thinks in the Irish way, tells me she has second sight. Fear goes through me when she says she has the power of an oracle, as though I feel she is looking over my shoulder at troubles to come. Christina foretold before the Pitt game that the Notre Dame team would be wearing their green jerseys, but she was wrong on the score. Her gift doesn't extend to guessing the sexes of babies waiting to be born. If I felt Christina was seriously clairvoyant, I would keep my distance from her. I am afraid of the Celtic kind of intuition called second sight. My Catholic grandmother was born, as the saying goes, with a veil, which was a sign she had special gifts. How could I tell if a ninety-year-old woman had second sight?

* * *

The prophecies of the Lord's birth in the Old Testament, Bible critics say, belong to the Christian imagination of St. Jerome, imposing meanings as he translated the ancient texts into the Latin Vulgate. At the sweet, solemn service called Vespers, we sing the messianic psalms. The Holy Spirit speaks to the Church through this liturgy of the word as we celebrate the salvation of God with the ancient poetry of Israel. At the "Hail, Holy Queen" (the prayers asking the Mother of God to turn her eyes toward us poor, banished exiles), I feel like a choir monk living in a long-ago time, keeping the calendar of the Church year. Thomas Merton wrote of his abbey at Gethsemani observing the liturgical cycle of seasons, created by monks out of an experience with the rhythms of the earth and the movements of the sun and moon, with long nights of sleep in the winter and briefer periods of rest in the summer when there is less darkness. Texts from the Vulgate were heard and seen everywhere in the abbey as reminders, Merton wrote, foretelling the Lord's coming, or proclaiming His feasts.

Now, I learn that the *Protoevangelium* — "I will put enmity between you and the woman, / and between your offspring and hers; . . ." (Genesis 3:15) — has nothing to do with *Evangelium*, proto- or otherwise. "The Lord said to my Lord: 'Sit at my right hand / till I make

61

your enemies your footstool' " (Psalm 110:1) is something different from the Messiah's enthronement in heaven. As seminarians, we were taken through the verses of the prophetic writings which were "proofs" that Scripture had known for hundreds of years that the Son of God would be born in Bethlehem, with kings from the east bearing him gifts. The "proofs" were looked on as a preamble, leading to the threshold of the Church, where, with the help of grace, we could make an act of faith in being Catholic.

Christian apologetics is not what it used to be. One of the first things to go after the changes of Vatican II were the "proofs" that were supposed to give us "moral-metaphysical certitude" of the faith we professed. Clear and logical proofs are hard to come by. Faith is a tug-of-war between the heart and the head. It seems to me the *informed* heart is most open to truth: the heart making the journey with the head, the head checking its reservations with the heart; logic keeping the emotions in tow, and the feelings bringing joy to an intellectual exercise.

I was raised to believe that the sacred texts lighted the way to faith. Faith, however, has a life and a will of its own, beginning and ending in mystery. The faith that you have been given illuminates the sacred text. "Therefore the Lord himself will give you this sign: the virgin shall be with child, and bear a son, . . ." wrote Isaiah (7:14). Textual criticism shows that he was talking about a young woman, with no thought in mind of a virgin birth.

The monk in his choir stall singing Vespers brings his faith in the Maiden Mother to his reading of Isaiah. The Scripture gives him the imagery of his prayer and praise. The inspired word is a lamp to his feet. It is the antiphon with which begins and ends his magnificat of assent. His faith is not as variable as the opinions of scholars.

Anna, welcoming the Child Jesus to the Temple, is recognizable from the women I have met at morning Mass. She is a touch of everyday life in the Christmas story; miraculous interventions are not part of my understanding of her. She was a woman advanced in years; I have seen her a thousand times in a Donegal shawl, lighting candles and saying the beads. She recognized that Mary's Child was destined for greatness in the kingdom of God. Along with Simeon, she had been waiting as widows often wait, postponing their deaths until after they have seen their children's children.

You wonder what an elderly person thinks about, living so long, left alone like the last leaf on the tree. An elderly woman, hugging her soul with tired arms, gets a look in her eye as though she were seeking eternity. Anna is called a prophet, which means she was endowed with an extraordinary gift of second sight. God may have blessed her with visions foreseeing all of redemption, but I suspect that any earth mother from Galway, with the gift of second sight, could have told you about the future of the little Boy Jesus.

My Catholic grandmother was older even than Anna, waiting in the Temple. She was a well-kept family secret, while I was growing up, as though she didn't exist. I rarely think of her except on December 15, when she is a memory connected with my father's death. I feel loyal, though it was too late to get close to this silent woman bent over with age. She hung pain in the air for my father with her Catholic piety. Anyone who knows what she said when she withdrew her blessing as a matriarch is now dead. My father must have hated my going to see her, though he never complained. I shouldn't be so nervous over maledictions, as though they represented a formula of destruction, because there are dark angels, full of iro-

ny, who overhear us talking. I blame my superstitious-
ness on the fact of being Irish, but it is probably more
primitive than Irish, like the attitude of the author of the
Book of Genesis.

My grandmother turned her face to the wall in grief,
after my father died. She did not live long enough to see
two of her grandsons ordained to the priesthood, but she
knew they were on their way. Like Simeon and Anna, she
may have felt it worthwhile to live so long a life.

All I can remember her saying was that I shouldn't
sing because my father had recently been buried.

A New Place In The Sun

It was the middle of Holy Week. Notre Dame had just
announced a new policy regulating the use of alcohol on
campus, and the students were in a feisty mood. Late one
night, about 1:30 A.M., they were rushing between buildings holding a protest rally, chanting "Give beer a
chance," and they were having the time of their lives. At
noontime, another rally was held. They occupied the cor-
ridors and stairways of the main building during lunch,
when the offices were closed, being careful to clean up
after themselves as they left. Football weekends used to
be this exciting at Notre Dame, and the peace demon-
strations for Vietnam were just as noisy. My dog Darby
O'Gill II, hearing the crowds run by, exploding fire-
crackers, wanted to join them. The cause was not worthy
of him, I pointed out. In Poland, the students were dem-
onstrating to save the crucifixes.

The world beyond the campus is going crazy. The
newspapers reported a mass murder in New York. The
CIA admitted it has been lying. In London, they shot at

people from an embassy. I got a box of Girl Scout cookies in the mail. At Mass, the songs of the Suffering Servant from Isaiah were being read. Cardinal Bernardin has been on television preaching forgiveness. He reminds me of my share of the world's guilt. I helped fill the bitter cup the Savior drank. All have sinned, and come short of the glory of God. As Kipling wrote, "Judy O'Grady and the Colonel's lady / Are sisters under the skin."

Yahweh described himself in Exodus as a jealous God. Jealousy is an active part of His love as the Master of the universe. He tells the Hebrews: "If you go tricking around with false gods, you and I are both losers. I'll go to the wall rather than give you up, because I love you so much." Jealousy, then, is tolerable, if you have credentials as the Alpha and the Omega. All other jealousy is self-destructive, and can ruin your day in the sun.

Jealousy is probably my worse fault as a priest. If I ever offer to drop out of the ranks of the ordained, I would give you excuses for not continuing as a priest: burnout, loneliness, or loss of faith. I hope my superior would be perceptive enough to ask: "What's the possibility you are feeling sorry for yourself because other guys are getting better deals?" The bottom line of a number of failed vocations is that one doesn't feel appreciated. Other fellows get all the recognition; they get the citations of merit at the testimonial dinners, the appointments to important committees with expense accounts, the promotions that will earn them even more public praise. I get left as the low man on the totem pole. Even if I remain in the system as a sneering cynic, I've taken the green-eyed monster to live with me as a housemate.

Jealousy is a secret vice, working like a termite to undermine the foundations of the house; it is the poison sickening the waters at the bottom of a life-giving well. I keep my jealousies well hidden — in conversations I'm not a sniper taking potshots. I play the game as a member of the team. Inwardly I'm angry, frustrated, and mean, waiting for the Peter Principle and Murphy's Law to bring the *Wunderkinder* to ruin so that I can look down with pleasure on their failures.

Jealousy is a rotten plank for a priest to walk on. The jealous priest is like the elder brother of the prodigal son who wanted the father to pay exclusive attention to him. He is like the servant who buried his single talent in despair, because his fellow servant had been given ten talents to play the market with. What can you do with a single talent when your rival has been given a small fortune for gambling wildly? (A talent is the equivalent of approximately a thousand dollars.) In being jealous, I'm saying: I want God to be honored, and the Church's work to get done, but I'll be happy only on the condition that I'm the chief tenor in the choir of praise, given the lion's share of the important chores. There is only one High Priest, whose instruments we are. Nothing done in His service is too humble to complain about, if only I could believe it.

I could never believe in a theology that told me my brother didn't make it to heaven. He was nine years older than I. He never had anything: education, money, marriage, a job he cared about, health. He wasn't religious in any noticeable way. I doubt that he was baptized. God must have made it up to him. We praise God with many titles: Father, Savior, Sanctifier. His image would be spoiled if He isn't fair. Some fundamentalists miss the point of love. It isn't just *me* the Savior loves; it's *us*. How can I say I love God, whom I don't see, if I don't love the brother I grew up with? Wherever we go, we go together as brothers; otherwise the trip is not worth making.

Someday, I will write something on the affection existing between brothers. Brothers, to begin with, have a world in common. One may outdistance the other; but there is no way of keeping score, to tell who is ahead. Between my brother and me, however, I think I was given a better chance of being happy.

Thomas Merton lost his brother, John Paul, as a casualty in World War II when his bomber crashed in the North Sea. John Paul had been given an accelerated course in Catholicism during his only visit to Gethsemani and was baptized just before going overseas, when Tom Merton saw him for the last time. John Paul was reported missing in action April 17, the end of Passion Week. Later, letters confirmed that on the fourth day after the crash they had buried John Paul at sea. Merton wrote a poem for John Paul: "For in the wreckage of your April Christ lies slain / And Christ weeps in the ruin of my spring. . . ."

Merton had a memory from childhood of the times he had gathered stones and chased John Paul away from the place where Tom and his friends were playing. "The picture I get of my brother is this: standing in this field . . . is this little perplexed five-year-old kid in short pants . . . afraid to come any nearer because of the stones, as insulted as he is saddened . . . he does not move . . . his tremendous desire to be with us will not permit him to go away. . . . The law written in his nature says he must be with his elder brother . . . he cannot understand why this law of love is being so unjustly violated. . . ."

Neither my brother nor I took the other along to the places we went. I couldn't have dragged him into my world if I had stoned him to death. I never played priest to my family, for fear I would come off as a phony. I was not a hero in the home where I grew up, but they liked me and were patient with my pretensions. My brother was a sweet-tempered man who never hurt anyone. I hurt him twice and he didn't deserve it. As a spoiled kid, turning on my brother, I violated the law of love. I can still see the look of disbelief on his face, just as Merton remembered the way John Paul watched him throwing the stones.

The first time, I struck him. He was just home from the hospital recovering from a head injury that had left a scar on his brain. My parents were there, sitting on the porch. My brother, pale and unsteady, teased me about the book I was reading. Enraged, I clobbered him on the cheek with my fist — the most physically violent act of my life — and I frightened myself with the horror because I realized I could have killed him. He transfixed me with his look of reproach. That beautiful, violated head could have been a model for a painting of the Suffering Servant before I ran off to escape the wrath of my horrified parents.

The second time, I was older. In his whole life, my brother had only one suit, bought for my grandparents' funeral, and I wanted it. It was a beautiful suit, double-breasted, tending toward dark blue, and it was almost my size. One day, without asking, I wore it to school. Coming home I fell and tore a hole in the right knee. I put the ravaged pants back in the closet without saying a word. Later, when my brother had seen the damage, I denied being responsible. "You must have fallen while you were drinking," I said, "and were too drunk to notice." He knew I was lying to save my skin. He was speechless with indignation with me for being such a bare-faced sneak willing to make him believe the worst about himself.

He knew me so well. I would have felt embarrassed,

later, to offer him my credentials as a shepherd, though we became very close. I felt praised when he showed that he regarded me as sincere. He was never a showboat like me; the evidence is there that he made his peace privately. Both of us, with the help of the other, will make it to heaven. The grace that the Lord gives comes to us as a family. Salvation, I hope, will turn out to be a family affair.

Every kind of jealousy diminishes our service to the jealous God. Jealousy masquerading as zeal diminishes the Church through the hidden sin, when one preacher discredits the other, casting doubts on his rival's openness to grace. Jealousy seems wistful when the old are jealous of the young, as when a father grows resentful at the undeserving children who have been given everything. Shakespeare tells us in *Cymbeline*: "Golden lads and girls all must, / As chimney-sweepers, come to dust." Some golden lads come to dust before their parents do, if we only knew. It is pathetic to be angry because youth is too wonderful to be wasted on adolescents.

On Good Friday, I read the Twenty-second Psalm, beginning: "My God, my God, why have you forsaken me. . . ?" Jimmy Swaggart says that the Lord recited this entire psalm as He was dying. How moving it would be to know for sure this was Christ's meditation: "I am like water poured out; / all my bones are racked. / . . . My throat is dried up like baked clay, / my tongue cleaves to my jaws . . ." (22:15-16). *Sitio*, He cried out, *I thirst*. The preacher can't tell us the excesses atoned for here. The image of the vicarious victim is etched on the mind. "He was pierced through for our transgressions. He was crushed for our iniquities."

How inappropriate it would be if someone yelled as though it were midnight, instead of the ninth hour: "Give beer a chance."

In the wreckage of our April Christ lies slain. As a sibling old enough to be their father, I am my brothers' keeper. Merton wrote for his brother:

> Sweet brother, if I do not sleep,
> My eyes are flowers for your tomb;
> And if I cannot eat my bread,
> My fasts shall live like willows where you died.
> If in the heat I find no water for my thirst,
> My thirst shall turn to springs for you, poor traveler.

All Of God's Children

In Houston I got a shoeshine at the stand in the hotel. The shoeshine boy said: "They ain't never been shined." What he wanted to say was: "They don't look worth shining." Of course they were worth shining: they were wingtip Florsheims, only two months old. Winter had taken its toll on them; they were scuffed lifeless from getting wet and drying out, and the outer soles had holes in them from wearing through. He made them look pretty good, but they would never be worth $108 again. That's how much they cost, plus $10 more for having the heels changed to rubber. I paid $118 for a pair of shoes I never took a brush to. I would never pay so much if I could get a decent fit in a cheaper shoe, so please don't scold me. I paid $1.50 for a shoeshine, and I tipped the boy as much again. His professional touch gave the Florsheims a second chance at life. I couldn't by myself get a miracle like that from Shinola.

The shoeshine reminded me of my father, who held strong opinions on lazy men and boys who neglected the care of their leather — and shoes didn't cost as much as

Tiffany's diamonds in his day. My mother gave me my first Bible; my father gave me a shoeshine kit and a safety razor so I wouldn't look like a bum. Shaving and shoeshines brought us very close as he got me ready for life. "After being scraped with a razor, the face should be splashed again and again with ice-cold water to eliminate the soreness," he told me, "and you'll never need shaving lotion." He lent me the Aqua Velva anyway so I'd smell good, as he did, to my mother.

He couldn't have imagined even John D. Rockefeller wanting to pay $118 for a pair of Florsheims. We didn't buy new shoes until they were absolutely necessary, because the country was in a depression. We took care of the shoes we had until they were complete ruins, being careful not to run them over at the heels; using a shoehorn, or the handle of a spoon as a substitute shoehorn, so we wouldn't break down the counters putting them on. Old shoes could be "tapped" a couple of times before throwing them away. When a pair was declared dead, in the opinion of my father, he would say: "Go see Abe Freedman on the way home from school."

Abe Freedman and my father had a traffic going on in covering the other's checks, to help the other (when money was short) from going out of business. As far as I could see, one would write a check, and the other would cover it. It was legal but chancey, and it worried them a lot. They never went to jail for taking advantage of the banks, and their businesses survived some pretty rough times. The closing of the banks in 1933 had come close to ruining my father; he had hundreds of dollars out in paper which he had to make good on. Abe Freedman was like a Jewish uncle protecting us from privations brought on the country by the foolishness of Roosevelt.

Thom McAns were like today's Florsheims com-

71

pared to Abe Freedman's shoes. He was a clothier cater-ing mostly to WPA employees and the out-of-work broth-ers-in-law of Pullman car porters, since his store was near the Union Station. His best shoes were made of im-itation alligator — in high yellow or black; the soles were made of cardboard. They gleamed nicely on a growing foot, though they were styled for an organ-grinder wan-dering the streets with a monkey. As a WASP, I deserved better, though it never bothered me to flash my way to school looking from the ankles down like Sportin' Life on the dance floor at the Elks' Club.

Looking back, I could guess we had our backs to the wall from the economical way we lived, though it never felt as though we were pinched by poverty. Rich doctors treated their own shoes the same way we did, my father explained, to get the most use. Rich doctors were no dif-ferent from the Griffins in buying ten-cent taps which were glued to the soles of new shoes before you wore them. The ten-cent taps stayed stuck until the first rain, when they started to loosen at the toe. The looser they got, the more they flapped, until finally, you had to be careful how you put your foot down, or you'd be tripped as though a large flappy tongue were loosely attached to your instep.

Ten-cent taps couldn't be glued on more than two or three times. You finally ripped them off because glue wouldn't stick to wet, papery soles. Six weeks' wear brought holes appearing under the ball of the foot you could put your finger through. Then you'd stuff the shoes with cardboard cut out of a cereal box. When the budget permitted it, you'd be ordered to see the cobbler, or to make another trip to Freedman's. The worst thing I ever did to my father was wiggling both my index fingers si-multaneously at him through the holes in the left and right soles of some worn-out shoes. My mother said it made him feel so bad he wanted to go out and hold up a bank. Abe's shoes were probably better than I'm describing them. My father took very good care of us. When other children went barefoot, we got acquainted with Abe's shoes. In winter, we had lumberman's boots or gum rubbers, bought at Liebowitz's on Saturdays after sundown when the Sabbath was over. The families living in Hooverville wrapped their feet in rags. Years later, after my father had died, I used to visit Abe at his store. He was a very kind man who showed me a lot of respect because he had loved my father so much. He would always give me a pair of socks as a present. Even his socks were too old for me. It's hard to describe socks that look like they've gone out of style.

By 1939, business had gotten better for my father. Besides, I had a job working to earn the money to buy my own clothes. Thom McAns were a bargain at $3.50 a pair, and they looked swell if they were oxblood red with a Blucher cut. Even then, I had trouble with cheap shoes because I was heavy, so my father took me shopping to buy me my very first pair of Florsheims, expensive at over $20 a pair. I wanted brown-and-white saddle shoes. My father showed me the difference between dress shoes and casual shoes. A person growing up responsible needs shoes to dress up in, he explained, to go with his good suit. Saddle shoes were too sporty for my needs, he felt, unless I planned to hold down a job as an ice-cream salesman.

We never had traditional father-and-son talks on the birds and the bees, but we bought shoes together. He handed down to me lessons on style which I felt he had inherited from his own father. These were rites of passage

73

initiating me into the wisdom that separates the man from the boy. My father was always surprising me with love, though he never knew how to talk about it. I got saddle shoes with red rubber soles for the summer after I graduated from high school.

For a while, my father's shoe size fit me. He would let me wear his shoes, but he wasn't crazy about the idea. He never liked my wearing other people's shoes, even his, because, he said, diseases are transmitted through the feet. Shoes are as private and personal as a toothbrush; neither should be accepted as hand-me-downs. Footwear shouldn't be lent between the two of us, because he was older and hosted an older person's germs. Yet, he would let me break in his new shoes for him, especially if I was wearing a new suit to impress a girl. He was taking a chance, because he knew my feet smelled from sweating. I borrowed my father's shoes only at times when I felt it was too cold for my feet to sweat.

Visiting my father's closet, I would notice he had saved a pair of damaged shoes, badly burnt out from friction over the toes, that had belonged to my brother. My brother, unconscious as he hung off the back of a car, had nearly gone to his death in these shoes. My mother had kept our baby shoes, bronzed as a remembrance, for sentimental reasons. My father had his keepsake too. His heart must have turned over every time he saw it.

The Notre Dame Glee Club sings a spiritual called "Shoes": "I got shoes, you got shoes, all God's children got shoes." Poor blacks would appreciate new shoes. A gambler shaking the dice intones for luck: "My baby needs new shoes." Before he can afford anything else, a father has to see that the kids' feet are kept warm. A boy growing up in a depression knows how quickly he wears out shoe leather with his running and jumping. "I got a harp," the Glee Club sings, and "I got wings." The shoes are more necessary than the harp or wings for walkin' over God's heaven all day.

In Houston, getting a shine, I thought: If my father saw the condition of these Florsheims, he would turn over in his grave. The shoeshine boy said: "You gotta nuther pair? If you leave these suckers with me, I can fix these ones up real good, if you got shoes for meanwhile." I got shoes. You got shoes. All God's children got shoes. We might have made a production number out of it if he had been Bill "Bojangles" Robinson. All the shoes I had were on my feet. I imagined that they wanted to walk away from me out of embarrassment. The tip I gave the boy was hush money. The best wax in Texas couldn't make those shoes as good as they used to be. Afterwards, I walked as tall as my father for the rest of the day.

Hands That Told Stories

My mother taught me to be attentive to hands, probably by making me conscious of my own. Of my ordination pictures, she preferred the ones where the hands were showing. "The hands are beautiful," she said simply.

Last Sunday evening, at a Mass I was attending in my mother's memory, I watched the priest's hands as he was preaching: the hand movements gave excitement to his language, as though the thoughts that stirred the brain reached down to the tips of his fingers. The hands were brown with summer sun, reminding me of birds playing around the stillness of a statue. If I could turn off the sound, I thought, and I were watching only the picture, the hands could tell the story by themselves.

During the liturgy, I admired the dignity given to

hands, obedient to the celebrant's voice, that bless bread and wine, and break the Host. It seemed to me that there is not a single sacrament where the hands are not necessary to signify the grace of Christ, so that if you are inattentive to what the hands are doing, you are inattentive to the sacrament itself. In Catholic spirituality, the hands should be given a chapter to themselves, titled "The Theology of Touch." In a faith that proclaims the Word made Flesh, the deepest, truest things human beings say to each other are affirmed when hands meet in signs of mutual support.

I learned to pay attention to my mother's hands. I could tell that she was worried if her hands were restless: folding and unfolding, wrestling against each other, because there was some thought her mind could not let go of. All her aging was in her hands. More than eighty years old, her voice was strong; her eyes were clear, and eventual blindness just made them brighter; and the years scarcely touched her face. The hands told the story: lovely as they were, they were an old person's hands, like veteran servants who have suffered and felt pain. Death only added to their dignity, with the plain golden wedding band and the crystal rosary identifying her as a Christian wife and mother.

I know how anxious the hands can get, having learned their language from my mother. I go to a party where I feel out of place, wishing I could have checked my hands at the door. I grab an hors d'oeuvre and a cocktail glass so that the other guests will not notice I'm ill at ease. I talk to a lady hanging on to a cracker and a glass, a stranger like me. Both of us would like to smoke cigarettes as an alternative to our life-support systems, but there are no ashtrays. It is impossible to step outside, because we're seventeen stories up.

Some showoff sits down at the piano to play, though nobody asked him to. The piano is out of tune, but he doesn't care. It's a way of coping with stress. The lady asks: "Do you play?"

"I have no talents involving manual dexterity," I reply. "As a child, I had to take a course in remedial nose-scratching." It's a joke, but I've caused her to worry. She's wondering if I suffered early polio.

Hors d'oeuvres, when you hang on to them, get soggy. I eat my cracker, because my index finger is sliding into the anchovy. The lady, getting the idea, joins me in munching. Suddenly, both of us have a free hand. No problem yet: she toys with a jewel at her throat; I jingle change in my pocket. After fifteen minutes, the drinks are gone too. We move to the refreshment table to re-stock. Curses! The plates are temporarily empty, and we can't get close to the bar. We have empty hands on our arms, flopping around like fish out of water. What to do?

"Would you like to see my grandchildren's pictures?" she asks suddenly.

"Delighted," I say. Once you've solved the logistics of keeping your hands busy, you don't have to smoke and drink at a party to have a good time.

* * *

A girl came into my room, crying. I had talked with her earlier, on her way out to supper. She's been dating a guy, now a senior. He had phoned to ask her to meet him. He had something important to say. She hoped he was going to give her a ring. He loved her enough to ask her to be engaged, she thought. It felt as though tonight might be the night.

Now, two hours later, I took her hands in my hands. She wasn't wearing a ring. She didn't want to talk, and I couldn't think of anything to say.

Finally, I asked: "Jack upset you?" She nodded yes. "He's met another girl?" She shook her head no.

Then, not believing her own words, she said: "He told me he wants to be a priest."

Her fingers were searching my hands for answers. My hands enfolded her hands, to offer apologies on behalf of the Church. In the ministry of comfort, the heart speaks its love with a touch.

* * *

A fox is just like a hundred thousand other foxes until you have tamed it, writes Saint-Exupéry. A rose is like a hundred thousand other roses until, by caring for it, you have made a certain rose unique. If you have met a little prince with gold hair in the African desert, he's just like a hundred thousand other little boys until you have established ties with him, saving him from dying of thirst and drying his tears. Later, when he has gone away, the wheat growing in the field, which is also golden, will bring you back the thought of him; and you will love to listen to the wind in the wheat. When you look at the sky, all the stars will be laughing, because on one of those stars, the little prince is laughing for you.

Of all the forms of language, because of my mother, I am attentive to the ways in which the hands speak, as unique as the tamed fox, the cultivated rose, the little prince who is tied to my heartstrings. Every time I notice that a preacher's hands are beautiful, I feel that my mother has told me something about the preacher. I touch hands that feel worn with work, or I sense pain in old hands crippled with arthritis, needing to be treated as gently as priceless china. I understand young strong hands that wear confidence like a glove. I touch with the tip of my fingers the rosebuds in a baby's fist. I promise to be protective of the young innocence that places itself with confidence in my own great hamhock mitts when I shake hands with a child.

I make a rough study of hands that are extended to me by people who paint, or heal, or sew, or teach, or beg, or ask help, or tell lies. I am my mother's son, believing that very often, before a word is spoken, the hands tell you the story, and honesty is tested by a touch. I couldn't care much for a person I would be embarrassed to shake hands with. I wouldn't feel on very sure grounds with a person embarrassed to shake hands with me.

It was in August of 1982 that I said good-night to my mother for the last time. I no longer remember clearly how she looked, though I know she was lovely. I remember her hands as I kissed them, and covering them with my own hands as I blessed them. I felt that in knowing what there was to know about those hands, I understood the truth about my mother. Her hands were so peaceful, fallen asleep in the shape of prayer.

The Mass, as far as I am concerned, is her poetry, as well as God's, more beautiful than the wind blowing golden notes in the wheatfield, or the bells, ringing in the sky as the stars laugh together in joy, because the little prince has come home. My mother couldn't be so close if she hadn't gone away. That is a comforting paradox belonging to the mystery of death.

CHAPTER 5

The Extra Sacrament

Two drunks went to a cemetery on a foggy night to look for Mulcahy's grave. After wandering around in the fog, they found the burial place. One of the drunks spelled out the name: Terence Mulcahy. The other drunk was staring at a statue of the Savior that Mulcahy's widow had put up.

After staring up at the sacred figure for several minutes: "Not a bloody bit like the man," says he. "That's not Mulcahy," says he, "whoever done it."

I've been rereading Joyce's *Ulysses* for the humor of the thing. The jokes and puns detach themselves from the pages, lodging themselves in the mind, useful for brightening up a homily if they are harmless enough. I wish I had the lilt of a brogue to show them off properly. Some people would take no pleasure in a story that mentions drunks. Irish stories are frequently indelicate; the more indelicate they are, the more Catholic they seem. Part of the fun of being a Catholic is knowing the difference between indelicacy and indecency. Belloc wrote the oft-quoted lines: "Wherever the Catholic sun does shine / There is always laughter and good red wine. . . ." Evangelists, burning with zeal, seem to be defective in their sense of the absurd. The preacher, angry with contemporary music, recites the titles of popular songs, and he breaks me up. "No-tell motel," spits out the preacher in disgust. To show you how far foolishness will go, he offers the lyric: "I don't want to go to heaven if there ain't no Mogen David wine." The preacher, who looks forward to seeing the golden streets, the gates of pearl, and the Apostle Paul, shakes his head in sorrow at the insult to Jesus. Mentioning the Mogen David title to a young Jesuit at dinner, I watched him "break his heart with laughter," as the Irish would say, at this trifle of amusement. One man's meat is another man's poison, although this doesn't explain the difference between a preacher and a Jesuit.

I grew up among people who always kept their sense of humor. I joined a church in which laughter is an extra sacrament, surpassing all the others in its power to heal. For thirty years, Catholics have argued about the changes in their ancient structure. I have an idea that the old Church exaggerated the truth of things. Doctrine and dogma, liturgy and spirituality, became cut and dried. In 1956, I heard complaints that Catholic theology was nearly stagnant.

Theologians were afraid to publish books advancing the development of doctrine because they were fearful of the watchdogs sniffing out heresies. Theology cannot stand still, it was explained, if it wishes to be living truth. The Church could not simply canonize creeds without reflecting on their implications. Theologians would not be credible as scholars if they were afraid to think out loud.

In 1956, these were some of the complaints the Catholic universities were making.

I am very fond of the Church I was ordained in; but for some time, I have felt as though I were present at the breaking up of a glacier, where everything was frozen in ice. The problem with glaciers is that they are of limited use to mankind. The Church wishing to be a servant of God needs to be more versatile than a glacier.

Irreverence is an intellectual exercise that an institution can't outlaw unless it wishes to set an inquisition up in business, or operate a death camp. This is the wonder of Joyce's *Ulysses*. Here was a young man who grew up in holy Ireland as it existed in the ice age of the Church. Fascinated by the dullness of dear, dirty Dublin, he turned the everyday life of this Catholic city into a parody and mock-heroic epic, never needing to invent the comedy because it was all there in the wit and irreverence of people drinking in pubs, arguing politics, and telling stories on their pious pastors. Joyce's own father had one of the most colorful gifts of gab in the country. My Irish mother, making plans, always relied on "the help of God and a few policemen." I figured the phrase was her own invention until I found it in Joyce as something he got from his father. It excites me to realize that my mother and Joyce's father drank at the same Irish spring.

Creeds and sacraments will endure until the end of time, but what is happening to the laughter that God handed down? It is no great sin to be irreverent, but it seems like a tragedy to be perpetually grim. I know priests who have become encrusted with bitterness. None of us would have survived our studies to be ordained if seminary life had not been redeemed by laughter. I had a master of novices who was a holy priest. His one great talent in training seminarians and brothers was that he could tell a joke. On the days he was grave, we could tell one another our own jokes on him. In my year and a day at the novitiate, the lesson I learned was that laughter is holy. The days and nights of silence, the hours of prayer, were mostly useful as a setting for the laughter. The laughter assured me I was still alive and young. Separation and segregation from the world in that lovely house, where forty of us lived, simplified me into understanding laughter as the great secret of God. As Chesterton says, Christ must have gone by himself onto the mountains to be alone with His mirth, because the Gospels never mentioned the days He laughed.

I used to be a celebrant with his back to the people. Now, at a Mass with a hundred other priests, the main celebrant stands with his back to us. We gave up Fridays as a day of abstinence, but students invite me to join them in meatless Wednesdays as a way of identifying with the hunger of the poor. On Sundays, a former beauty queen in a sequinned pantsuit stands by my side as a eucharistic minister while I am also distributing Communion; in the old days, veiled nuns needed an indult to wash the sacred linens. I knew over a hundred ways of committing mortal sins in saying Mass. Now that those mortal sins have been repealed, I keep meeting liturgists more intolerant than Fortescue and Wapelhorst, those choreographers of the Roman rubrics. The Sunday Mass, lacking the terseness of Latin, seems so wordy, so bland and full of redundancies, so deficient as an adventure of sailing to Byzantium, though it is my own fault. I didn't mind going flat while singing a preface, when the flatness was hidden by a dead language; but in English, the mistake is conspicuous enough for the cantor to upstage me.

An alternative for feeling sorry for myself is laughter at the honest expense of pretensions and pomposities. *In vino veritas*, they say. In laughter too there is *veritas*.

I am not worried because there is no one alive in the world today capable of writing a Catholic novel with the greatness of *Ulysses*. It bothers me that probably no one wants to write an updated *Ulysses*, because no one cares enough to get the absurdities together as an art form. I've not read enough to know if there is a Protestant equivalent of *Ulysses*. I doubt that there could be. A writer-friend of mine claims the age of Catholic satire is over, because the things that were satire are now the norm.

We could have destroyed Hitler if we had laughed at him soon enough. We waited until he was dangerous, and then our ridicule infuriated him. If Adam and Eve had laughed at the snake, we'd still be on Easy Street. Armageddon itself could be avoided, if leaders remember to laugh in time. It would be silly to pretend that if clowns, meeting at a peace table, offered to make jokes instead of war, the bombs would go away. Yet men are never more reasonable than when they are sincerely laughing; laughter distinguishes man from the beast. I'm not more intelligent in the things I do than Darby O'Gill II is in the things he does. I'm not more loyal, patient, or loving than that cocker spaniel is, but I have a better-developed sense of humor. In the eternity God has planned for us, a fringe benefit will be that He will share His jokes.

As members of a grace-bearing institution, we could investigate whether taking oneself too seriously was part of the original sin. Adam and Eve were deceived by the promise that if they disobeyed, they should be as gods. Being as gods was what they were willing to settle for. I don't want to be as celebrated as a god, so long as my convictions as a fundamentalist Catholic or a born-again liberal are respected as infallible; with the education and experience I've got, I couldn't be wrong. It seems a little godlike to be so right. I went to school run by nuns; this is what they taught, and they knew the truth. I took theology courses in college, and we read the encyclicals, so don't try to pull the wool over my eyes. I read it in the Catholic paper in an article written by Father Jones, a very smart priest who knows what the pope thinks, and has been to Fatima. St. Paul writes: "Now we see indistinctly, as in a mirror" (1 Corinthians 13:12). The Church becomes so dreary when Catholics camp out in anger.

* * *

An old, old man was planning to be married. The priest asked why he wanted to be bothered. He said in a worn-out voice: "At least there'll be someone to answer the Rosary."

On hearing this, how could you explain to a Baptist the pleasure that tickles you?

Cold Turkey

Mark is a Notre Dame senior who keeps trying to help me stop smoking. Sunday morning, at breakfast in the dining hall, he sat there, with the sweet rolls between us, stroking his beard, and musing about how much it would help me if I gave up cigarettes. I found his arguments insipid.

"Mark," I said, "please. No more portrait of the reformer as a young wimp. Not before the second cup of coffee."

He made persuasive noises with his mouth as though he were trying to transmit subliminal language off the ends of his moustache. He takes himself very seriously; when he's being most difficult, he fixes his shaggy face into expressions learned from the Man of LaMancha hearing himself called to an impossible dream. I'm never patient with him in the morning when he seems to be listening to inner voices which are waiting for me to say yes.

"What are you doing this summer?" I said, as I lit a Pall Mall. I had a fear that he would answer that every morning of June, July, and August, he would wake up telling himself: "This is the first day of the rest of my life."

"I'll keep busy," he said, sounding like an embodiment of the Protestant ethic. "Maybe I'll get a job with the Catholic Worker. It would do me good to see the real world." This is another idea he has, that one world is more real than another. If he lives long enough, he'll find that every world has its own share of pain. The Catholic Worker Movement, I think, is not so much the real world as a half world, where the burnt-out cases come to get soup.

"Why not get a job in a hospital," I suggested, "as an orderly?" Kids wanting to serve the real world, it seems to me, often end up in projects where they build tennis courts for slum kids in Latin American countries. They feel cheated by the experience.

"That's a good idea," he said. "In the fall, I'll be attending graduate school, studying dramatics."

"In New York or New Haven?" I asked. I knew he had applied to Columbia and Yale.

"In Washington," he said. "I've decided to stick with Catholic education."

He didn't make it into Columbia or Yale, I thought. "That's nice," I said. "You'll like Washington."

"My best teachers have always been nuns and priests," he said.

"You're still arguing," I said.

"Try it for half a day," he said, "for twelve little hours." He sat there coaxing me with the ends of his whiskers.

"If I stop smoking for half a day," I said, "will you promise me to shave?"

"You're on," he said. "You can keep an hourly journal."

This is the journal I kept of the Great Smokeout, Sunday in Eastertide, 1982.

8:30 • Matches and cigarettes were removed from my control. Ashtrays were emptied of butts, which were flushed away to a watery grave. Furniture and clothing were searched for the humblest crumb of tobacco. Mark would have examined my closets and drawers, if I hadn't reminded him I was on my honor to go cold turkey for the next twelve hours.

8:55 • I had a valedictory smoke, as final as a last sacrament.

9:00 • The smokeout begins.

9:05 • I grew edgy, and Mark offered me a sack of peppermints, which I refused out of respect for my fillings.

9:15 • I ate my first peppermint.

9:25 • I told Mark to get out, because he made me nervous with his watching. After he left, I searched the room again, finding matches in the corner of the couch. I got change for a dollar, for emergency use in the cigarette machine in case of a nicotine fit. I read Prospero's speech from the *Tempest*: "Now have our revels ended. . . ."

10:00 • Mark reappeared, offering to read me excerpts from the U.S. surgeon general's report. I called him an insensitive idiot, and excused myself with vehemence to prepare a sermon. From then until the end of Mass, I kept busy with God's work. I noticed I was beginning to twist my toes, pushing them hard against the tops of my shoes; probably, I thought, the first sign of a nervous breakdown.

12:00 • I had lunch with some fussbudgets who usually avoid me at table because I'm a smoker. Their conversation was dead, dull, and dreary. I realized that all these years, tobacco has been my defensive weapon, to keep the bores away.

1:00 • Kept an appointment with a girl, depressed because her boyfriend had left her. "Have a peppermint," I said. "It will help a little." She thought I was crazy. "You don't understand," I wanted to shout. "I've lost a close friend of my own!" She finally left, disappointed. I knew my counseling skills were gone. I felt like an old man, fallen, like Macbeth, into the sere and yellow leaf. Everything seemed to have died except my lively toes, which kept marching to the beat of a different drummer. My dog licked me with his tongue, like the mongrels that comforted Lazarus. I fell asleep, exhausted from the toes down. I dreamed that Lucky Strike green had gone to war.

3:00 • Mark came in for a progress report. "You're breathing better," he said. "With the time half over," I said, "I have a right to insist you shave half your face." He said: "For you, it's a matter of life, or breath." I threw him out. Then I checked my change in the cigarette machine, to make sure the coins were dependable.

3:00-5:00 • I tried to keep busy, but my heart wasn't

in it. My mind drifted in and out of attention spans. "I can't go on like this," I thought. "I'm wasting my life." I found myself grieving, as though a letter had come bringing sad news from home.

5:00 • I walked the dog. I sucked in air that was allegedly clean, and felt dizzy. I reached for a peppermint; the sweetness made me gag. "Old maids," I thought, "living in lodgings, die like this, rotting out their throats with sugar."

6:00 • Before dinner with the religious community, I refused a drink. One good habit supports another, I thought; one foolish denial corrupts the world. My brain signaled its regrets to my toes, already in a panic, trying to braid themselves together for mutual support. The superior noticed I was sweating. "A touch of malaria," I explained, "from my time in the bush." He thought I was being silly from too much to drink. I wondered if he would send me a note.

7:00 • The long day was ending. In an hour, I would buy Pall Malls, leaving them in plain sight for Mark to see. I felt good. Cold turkey had turned out to be a piece of cake. I started the countdown until nine o'clock.

8:55 • Mark dropped by to say he was on his way to Chicago, to meet his parents. In the morning, he said, I could go with him to the barber. I no longer felt vindictive toward hairy apes. I said: "What business is it of mine how you treat your face?" He grinned sheepishly and with genuine gratitude.

9:00 • My hour of victory. Lady Nicotine was back. A gentleman never keeps a lady waiting. I've been faithful to the wench for thirty years, I thought. It's her turn to wait for me.

10:15 • I finally broke the cellophane. I had remembered to bring matches from supper. With the ease of a veteran observing a familiar ritual, I lit up. The first draw was nice, and I inhaled again. Suddenly, I felt like a disenchanted lover whose romance has begun to fail.

I had to coax my throat not to burn, and my stomach to resist nausea. It was like the very first time, when, as a boy, I wanted the sophistication of being a smoker, Cole Porter-style, against all common sense of the body's warning systems.

It took three cigarettes to get the old smoothness back. By the time I lit up for the fourth time — around 10:45 — I could have given Marlboro men a run for their money. But I was no longer sure I would rather fight than switch.

That was yesterday. Today, again, I'm not smoking. Tomorrow, I may buy another pack of cigarettes. Tomorrow, anything can happen. Tomorrow, as Mark, sounding wimpish, might say, is the first day of the rest of my life.

A New Year's Carol

The Johnnie Walker was dead; there was no doubt about that. It had been killed the night before at an end-of-the-year party. Yet, coming into the room, I had mistaken it for a full bottle, an unopened gift from the Ladies' Sodality. I've never wept over a dead soldier. The liquor had pleasantly served a social need as an encouragement to good conversation. I've never been ambitious to stock a bar; now, at year's end, I wanted to clean house. I didn't need friends coming in, arguing into the early hours of January 1, keeping old John company. I was pleased that the bottle was dead. I felt bothered by the fleeting impression that I had an untapped jug on my hands.

I settled down in my easy chair with the *TV Guide*, looking for an old movie. Fools and their money were being soon parted, I thought, in expensive clubs with package deals. Paper hats and champagne at fifty bucks a member were a humbug. Winning the West with John Wayne was as much entertainment as I needed. At midnight, the station would switch to Times Square and, after that, to the Waldorf Astoria, where Guy Lombardo's orchestra would be playing my kind of music. At 12:30, I would say my prayers and go to bed. By day after tomorrow, the world would be back to its own grim business as usual, surviving the winter and waiting for the Super Bowl. I was looking forward to snowstorms in January. I was tired of being bored by Christmas.

I must have fallen asleep. I awoke with the feeling I was being stared at. The television was off; the reading lamp was dim. Sitting across from me was a figure of old appearance that I immediately identified as a specter.

"Jacob Marley?" I asked politely.

"Johnnie Walker," he replied. "Black Label."

"We were never really close," I said. "I rarely gave you house room. Why have you come?"

"The ghost of Hamlet's father is in Denmark," he said. "You've not yet given me a decent burial." He motioned toward the empty fifth on the coffee table, waiting to be thrown out with the party debris.

"I must be dreaming," I said. "Too rich a diet is the ruin of sleep."

"You'd be smarter examining your conscience than the contents of your stomach," he said. "Look here!" Lifting a fleshless arm, he rattled a paper chain that was unsettling to my mind. "Broken promises," he said reproachfully. Extending his diaphanous legs, through which I could see the rug, he groaned: "Unkept resolutions. These are the shackles that belong to your soul. Johnnie gets to wear them as the companion who aided your weakness.''

"Old demon drink," I said sternly, in an exorcist's voice, "go about your business with lushes and winos. You were never a problem to me. One more insulting word, and I'll lay holy water on your tail. I'll kick you downstairs with the sign of the cross." Seeing gloom deepen in that face belonging to the grave, I added in a more kindly way: "Because I thought we were friends, I've always spoken well of you."

He struggled to his feet. "Consider me the truth at the bottom of the glass," he said. "Before morning, you will have three visitors: the ghost of New Year Past, the ghost of New Year Present, and the ghost of New Year Yet To Come." He rattled his chains for a last time. *"In vino veritas,"* he said. "Have a good evening."

He retreated toward the television until he was finally swallowed up by the picture tube, leaving dead memories hanging in the air. All at once, Johnny Carson was on the screen, talking with Rodney Dangerfield. I kept thinking of paper chains that reminded me of unread copies of *War and Peace*, study guides (for a course in conversational Spanish) I had sent away for, letters exchanged with the guestmaster at Gethsemani about a retreat I never made, and an Adidas box with my jogging shoes on the floor of my closet.

I decided to greet New Year's in bed, listening to "Auld Lang Syne" on the clock radio. I said my night prayers standing up, because the floor was cold. I set the alarm late, so I would miss Morning Prayer. I hunkered down under the blankets, with cigarettes and an ashtray on the nightstand, in case I got nervous in the middle of the night. I closed my eyes, hoping to sleep well.

Suddenly, I heard an airline hostess, the ghost of New Year Past, announcing: "Fasten your seat belts, please, with seats and trays in an upright position. Thank you for flying the friendly skies of United." When I opened my eyes, I was seated in a theater, where Ralph Edwards was emceeing a production of *This Is Your Life.* A young man was onstage, wearing the scared look of the newly ordained. Ralph Edwards was saying: "For your work as a scholar, your friends want you to have this Greek lexicon and Hebrew dictionary. For your future service to the Church, please accept this golden miter made for you by the arthritic hands of cloistered nuns." Offstage, I could hear my mother's voice repeating her early advice: "If you insist on being a priest, Robert, please do it right and become at least a bishop."

To the "March of the Siamese Children," two little China people brought the new priest a wooden bowl, as the emcee explained: "For your meals in the rice paddies as a missionary in China, continuing Gregory Peck's work in the *Keys of the Kingdom.*" The next gift was a pipe like Bing Crosby's as Father O'Malley. Mickey Rooney himself, taking time off from being Judge Hardy's son, handed over the deed to Boys Town, while Spencer Tracy intoned on tape: "There's no such thing as a bad boy."

Ralph Edwards's voice rose to a crescendo of excitement as he described the washer, dryer, and freezer stuffed with TV dinners that the program's guest would take home, until an announcer's voice broke in, saying: "Wrong program. You've just switched scripts to *Queen for a Day.*"

Then I was back in bed again, with the digital clock registering 1:00 A.M. I lit a cigarette. I wasn't too upset.

Those dreams were all dated, belonging to pre-Vatican II.

The ghost of New Year Present turned out to be a transit cop on the New York subway. "Walk upstairs," he said. "The doctor is waiting."

The doctor said crossly: "You're putting on weight again, and you continue to smoke. How can I help you, if you don't take care of yourself?"

A strong man cringes, even in a vision, at a scolding from his cardiologist. Bill collectors have to accept your word that there's a check in the mail. Confessors owe you the courtesy of an absolution, if you promise them an amendment of life. Only doctors are merciless when you meet them in bad dreams. "Expect a call from the undertaker soon," my doctor said. "In your lifestyle, you've made your own arrangements with the avenger of the social vices."

The Christmas cheeses have ruined me, I thought. I can take ten-mile walks, fasting from sunrise to sunset. Offer me a cracker that's been spread with Kraft's, and I become programmed for gluttony, springing at the hors d'oeuvres table as though Vienna sausage were an alternative to torture.

"Yond' Cassius has a lean and hungry look," I defend myself with a customary witticism. "Let me have men about me who are fat."

In my vision, I see a fallen prophet, reeking of anchovies, who once sneered at John the Baptist for spoiling his disposition with locusts and wild honey. My doctor's voice breaks in: "It took the mother of a dancing girl to do John in. He wasn't his own worst enemy."

Back in my bedroom, going to the closet shelf, I took down the fruitcake that had been mailed from the pastry chef at the Plaza. Crumbling it with my hands, I flushed it down the toilet. Smelling the odor of spices and candied fruit on my fingers, I washed my hands with Ivory soap. My guide on the vision of New Year Yet To Be turned out to be my own cocker spaniel, Darby O'Gill II. I followed him across the Notre Dame campus, through the grotto, past the lakes, into the community cemetery. Stopping at a grave, as yet unmarked with a stone, Darby buried a bone he had brought as a gift to the dead. Then, slinking away, he ran into the traffic of a busy street. I understood then that in my warning dream, my only survivor had become a street dog, an inner-city mutt. Eventually, the dogcatcher would get him. A sentimentalist would bring him home from the city pound, and turn him into a lap dog. So cracks a noble heart.

January 1, I woke up late. The morning was gray. Notre Dame wasn't playing in a bowl game. None of the signs were hopeful. I made a breakfast of cold mince pie, because I hate miraculous conversions. The ghosts of time had finished their business. I made a resolution never to drink Johnnie Walker. Otherwise, the New Year wouldn't change a thing.

CHAPTER 6

The Avenues Of Babylon

In New York, I spend too much time by myself. Some days it may be noontime, when I'm saying Mass, before I talk to anyone. Some evenings, from seven until bedtime at two or three in the morning, I am alone, wondering what to do with the time. Some nights, I walk the streets, stopping at bookstores, looking in store windows, needing some place to go for an hour's conversation. On the hottest evenings, I start reading after supper, promising myself that I will look around the neighborhood when the air gets cooler. At 11:00 P.M., I force myself to a decision to stay in, because I could get hurt on the street if the crazies are out; I could be surprised by violence while eating an ice-cream cone, if some nut takes a dislike to me. I am not really afraid of strangers. I am simply bored by the thought of local color, and I'm too lazy to want to take a walk on trash-filled sidewalks.

On lonely evenings, I keep waiting for something to happen.

The city seems to be waiting for something to happen. A whole crowd of us are like the people waiting in the subway for a train to come. The transit authority has no contract to service this line. No schedule has been posted to say if the train will ever come. Still, we wait, alternating between hope and despair, looking and listening for the cars that will take us to another, better place.

It helps to have money in your pocket. You could never have enough money to buy your admission into the clubs night after night. By yourself, what entertainment could you find in the clubs? You could watch, not daring to get involved even if you were asked. The decencies you have chosen to be faithful to do not encourage you to mingle with the swingers. You could pay your way into the movies, but you would quickly grow tired of spending your time with *Superman III* and *Octopussy*, even if the theaters were open after midnight.

One night I went to an all-night movie on Forty-second Street to see the *Wiz*. I was the only white person in a crowded theater. A woman next to me borrowed a match to light a joint. The man in back of me was also smoking pot. I began to get a headache from the fumes. I was afraid even to go into the restroom. It was only nine in the evening, and the audience was comparatively sedate. If I feared the behavior in the green wood, what outrages might I expect in the dry? On Forty-second Street, they cheer the guys in the black hats.

Not too long ago, on an early Saturday evening, an old lady phoned the rectory. "I'm eighty-four," she said. "Alone here in this apartment, I got frightened. I thought if I had someone to talk to, it would help me get my bearings."

Ten minutes later, when she let me in, she asked if I was a policeman. When I told her I was a priest answering her call to the rectory, she explained: "I can't see well. My eyesight is very poor."

She had lived alone for two years, since her sister died. She had moved to this apartment on Washington Place in the year I was born. The lady upstairs looked in on her sometimes, but the eighty-four-year-old woman said she hated to bother the neighbors.

"A little while ago, I felt frightened all of a sudden," she said. "I don't know why I was frightened. Maybe it was the thought of death, but I'm used to death. Do you think that I'm losing my mind?"

I assured her she was not losing her mind. "Have you seen or talked to anyone today?"

"Are you a policeman?" she asked again. "I can't see well enough to tell if you are a policeman."

I introduced myself again, and asked: "Have you been alone all day?"

"I've been alone since my sister died," she said. "I'm very careful with the gas." Her hands were nervous in a way my mother's hands used to be nervous.

"How long since you've eaten?" I asked.

"I don't remember. I'm not very hungry, but I suppose I have food if I wanted to eat." I thought she was going to show me her kitchen. Instead, she started to sort blindly through some papers on the table.

"It would be terrible if I lost my mind," she said. "Do you think I should be in the hospital?"

On a Saturday evening in New York, what can you do for a lonely old lady confused in her mind? You don't want to send her to the hospital; the sick, disturbed people she would see there would unhinge her completely. Instead, you spend time with her and make sure that she eats, and then you find someone to keep an eye on her when you've left. It helps your conscience to learn that a very caring nun visits the old lady every day, bringing her a meal. Often, I was told, when the old lady gets frightened, she calls the rectory for help. It's no extraordinary thing for the priests to pop in to see her. Having battled loneliness myself, it frightened me to see how bad loneliness can get. She was still asking if I was a policeman when I left. It was not easy for her to tell because, as she explained to me, her eyes were not that good anymore.

The problem with loneliness is that you can almost get used to it. During a recent summer, I spent a lot of time with the New Testament. St. Paul, it seems, must have loved Jesus more deeply than any other Christian who ever lived. The most worthwhile project of a lifetime is to learn to love the Lord nearly as much. After an hour with Paul, it is hard to come down from the mountaintop. I feel the words locked inside me; it is difficult to find thoughts for a conversation. As a preacher, I am tongue-tied; at table, I'm a bore, full of convictions having nothing to do with the latest Woody Allen movie everyone is talking about.

It is dumb to let habits of solitude make you into a closet Catholic, sitting in an air-conditioned room, reading textbooks on Christology. It is only a twenty-minute walk from the rectory to Penn Station. The devil does business in front of Penn Station, and God seems an eternity away. God so loved the world that He gave His only begotten Son. Would the crowds believe you if you said this at Penn Station? In New York, there are domestic truths that sound true in church, and street truths known to the jungle; and the crowd can tell you the difference. The street truth about God is that He either doesn't care, or He does not exist. If I were in the crowd's place, I might be just as cynical. It must be hard to believe in Christ when you've grown up in a world that sends you to bed hungry.

A young girl with a microphone stridently scolds passersby because of their sins: "You need someone to die for you. Without the shedding of blood, there is no remission of sins." Is this what the Gospel means? I wonder. To the crowds at Penn Station, the crucifixion of Jesus is another example of how the good die young.

I've been told by some that I'm a cynical priest who discourages vocations by my lack of faith. One great, overwhelming gift the Lord permits me to use as His gift to sinners: He lets me say Mass every day. In the heart of darkness, He lets me say Mass; in the valley of death, I offer the Church's sacrifice. All the beat-up lives, all the lonely people, have Christ, the great high priest, interceding for them in a liturgy of earth shadowing heaven, as He offers himself in sacrifice, as described in the Epistle to the Hebrews. On every skid row you find priests keeping the memory of Calvary fresh and green and life-giving in the experience of the Church; for all the shabby losers, love is here from the heart of Christ.

The Manhattan moon, bathing the tops of buildings with its ethereal light, seems a lot closer than usual. Everywhere you lift your eyes, the beauty of towers and bridges seems worthy of an enchanted island. The streets are a different story, like the avenues of Babylon.

Millions, priests included, work to save the city. How can you feel so isolated in a place you share with so many?

Easy Mark

I don't want them mistaking me for an easy mark. Giving away money is no problem, if I have money. Giving away money is easier than trying to figure out the truth of a sob story. The sob stories I hear in a New York rectory usually try to take a bite out of my folding money. Whatever the promises of repayment, I never see the money again, and that leaves me with the feeling that I've been lied to. It's one of the risks of my profession. It's easier to say good-bye to money than it is to figure out if I'm dealing with a chiseler. Nineteen times out of twenty, I end up as a con artist's victim. I don't want them to think it's too easy. I always warn them: "I know you may be lying." I wonder if they chuckle at my naïveté as they leave the rectory?

Gentleman John said he was fifty-seven, and an excon (a former professional football player who had served twenty years for transporting counterfeit money). "The judge made an example of me, and I served every year of the sentence in prisons of the South."

Coming out of the pen, he found himself living in a "different world." He said the three bad breaks of his life were doing time, coming down with epilepsy, and being robbed in New York. He deserved prison, he told me; the other two disasters, he insisted, were because the cards were stacked against him.

He was tired of the struggle. He had two weeks' pay waiting for him in Connecticut. Travelers' Aid wouldn't lend him the carfare to go to New England and collect his pay. As an old athlete, he could go to the sportswriters and tell them his story. All the sportswriters would know who he was. To tell the truth, he hated sportswriters, and didn't want to get into their clutches because they could ruin a player. He wouldn't appeal to the sportswriters. He refused to become a bum on the Bowery. He was feeling ill with the flu. He was tired of the struggle. He had decided that the only soution was to do away with himself.

"Are you telling me," I said, "that if I give you eleven dollars for train fare, you'll go to Connecticut, and collect your pay? If I don't give you eleven dollars, you'll do away with yourself?"

He didn't want it to sound that way, he said. He knew it seemed like he was telling me that, but I should not misunderstand him. He was thinking the matter out, and needed counseling. He was tired of living with his back to the wall. He was ready to give up, and wanted to be counseled.

I thought: I'm the one who should have suggested counseling. He had stolen my thunder. Gentleman John knew his dance steps as well as I did.

He may have been an ex-Detroit Lion, down on his luck. He may have had two college degrees, and been an ex-con, without a set of teeth, with two weeks' pay waiting in Middleton, Connecticut, from his job as a forklift operator at Pier 8. Who wanted to check his story for the sake of eleven dollars? I wouldn't waste my time counseling him until he had given proof he was sincere.

He stood up suddenly, as though he were headed for the exit, but he only needed to fill the unused space in the room. "I wanted to talk matters over," he said, pacing. "I'm sorry to bother you. I didn't know where else to go to see a priest. I've reached the end of beating my head against the wall. I'm not asking for anything."

He kept excusing himself as a nuisance wasting my time. His ploy worked, because I felt defensive with guilt. He was a slick operator, keeping me on the edge of my chair for fear he would bolt before I could help him. He was blackmailing me with his threat of suicide. You can't argue with the threat of suicide if it's being used to manipulate you. You can say: "Go ahead and kill yourself," and take your chances. You start living with the dread that you've made a spectator sport out of Russian roulette.

Part of the cosmic craziness is that discouragement can push one of life's victims over the edge. In a pain-filled, vulnerable moment, the need for eleven bucks can be the straw that breaks the camel's back. I knew a student who traced lines over his jugular vein because his car wouldn't start on a winter morning. New York City is famous as a place offering you the final indignity, refusing you the train fare to Middleton, Connecticut.

I may have been a fool, but I gave Gentleman John his money without putting him through an inquisition or asking to check his papers. There's one chance in ten thousand that I saved him from final despair. For eleven dollars, I could afford the odds. I told him I'd been lied to before. He said, "Sure, but not by me." The ex-con went off with eleven dollars, safe from the clutches of the sportswriters, with me shouting "Good luck!" at his back going out the door. I have seen neither hide nor hair of him since.

* * *

One New Year's Eve, I went with friends to Brooklyn for dinner at a landmark restaurant. At midnight, we were in Manhattan at the fountain in front of the Plaza, sipping champagne from paper cups. The sky lit up over Central Park; I wasn't sure if it was fireworks or the Second Coming of the Lord. Fortunately for me, the city was showing off the skyrockets. For fifteen minutes on a cold night, the falling stars celebrated the New Year as though it were the Fourth of July.

At the entrance of the subway, street people bundled up in rags stretched out on the concrete in whatever places of warmth they could find. It is shocking to see anyone, especially old ladies, without a decent place to sleep. Money is usually in short supply in the winter. Any problem that can be solved with money, I have glibly remarked, is not much of a problem: for example, you can't buy your way back from the grave, or unplug the systems that sponsor the Bomb by writing a check. How many dollars would you need to thrust into a derelict's hand as an apology for his indignity of being homeless? Parties with horns and paper hats were going on at the Waldorf Astoria for over a C-note a head. In the subways under Fifth Avenue, there was no "Auld Lang Syne" among aging ragamuffins, nor was there gratitude among them for fireworks in the park. The New Year's champagne turned to vinegar in my stomach from the uneasiness of social guilt.

* * *

A man on Forty-fourth Street asked me for a cigarette when he saw me smoking. "I'm sorry," I murmured, because I was afraid I would have to touch him, or be touched.

"I understand," he said pleasantly enough to make me cringe. "Thank you very much, sir, and have a good evening."

Outside the rectory, a black man asked: "Can you spare some change?"

"I don't have any change," I replied. In my pocket, I felt a fistful of change, which I wordlessly gave him, to his surprise and pleasure.

At Grand Central Station, a strange little gnome quarreled bitterly with the ticket agent. The gnome was cashing in the unused half of a round-trip ticket costing twelve dollars. He was getting back only four dollars instead of the six he was expecting. I was standing in a long line of people who had trains to catch. I wanted to give him the two dollars so that I could buy my ticket to a fireplace in Westchester, where I would be spoiled with treats. I was afraid of incurring the instant hatred of the bearded stranger complaining of the injustices of the railroad. On the train, two querulous women began bad-mouthing the conductor when he told them they owed four dollars more if they wanted to ride to Tarrytown. One of them mentioned what she would do if she could get her hands on the ticket clerk. The other described the ticket seller in unpleasant terms. "We haven't got the money, so what are you going to do?" the first woman asked. The conductor shook his head. "You can't get blood out of a couple of tough turnips," he must have been thinking. I was ready to pay the extra fare if they started to wipe up the train with him.

In a restaurant the next day, I ordered quiche with broccoli and mushrooms. The waitress served the quiche, putting it down, then picking it up and smelling it. "What's the matter?" I asked.

"It smells funny," the waitress said. "How does it taste?"

I was no longer hungry enough to find out. "It looks fine," I said. She shrugged her shoulders, and again gave the quiche the evil eye. As soon as she left I picked up my check, paid the cashier, and left the restaurant. At least I had a cup of coffee. Only Caspar Milquetoast pays for food he hasn't eaten. It's more classy to be an easy mark than to hassle over money.

* * *

My New York cardiologist tells me my heart size is back to normal. Modern science has looked at the blood specimens; white-gowned lab workers say that healing has taken place. Everything is as it should be, and my heart is in the right place. We're discontinuing the digitalis, the doctor says. The beat no longer needs strengthening with drugs. There is no clinical evidence that my heart is any bigger than anyone else's.

My priest-friend from Cleveland says I shouldn't have given Gentleman John more than five dollars: "He would have been happy, and you wouldn't feel like an easy mark." God is praised by our alms to the poor. I'm thankful for my health and other blessings. Notre Dame brought home a victory from the Liberty Bowl. Maybe I helped Jerry Faust win one for the Gipper by being kind to an ex-con who used to play football for a professional team.

Trivial Pursuits

Peter is a panhandler. He sits in front of the church every day asking for money. He puts his arm in a sling and covers his head with a bandage, as if he had been kicked by a horse. He really is a pathetic-looking figure. The head bandage covers the earphones of his Sony Walkman. He removes the earphones when he wants to talk to you. His arm no longer seems broken when his workday is over. Panhandling is how he makes his living, and he thinks of himself as a professional.

One evening he told me, as he sat there counting dollar bills, that he had made over sixty dollars from his day on the street. I told him that by flashing a bankroll, he was ruining his image as a bum. He said: "What do I care? I got it from tourists I will never see again." He had played his little game with the weekend trade; now he was being his hard-nosed self. He didn't have to put on his act for me. He wasn't ashamed to let me see how much of a fake he is. I began to feel like an accomplice to his cheating. The next day he hit me up for a dollar so that he could get supper. He still had enough money for the meal, but he needed the dollar as a tip.

Peter practically belongs to the parish, and all the priests like him. He shows up for Sunday Mass, and is asked to leave when he isn't clean. The pastor has forbidden him to bring up the gifts when he is shoeless with dirt streaked over his feet and looking like a wild man. He makes the parishioners nervous when he looks so dirty. Something tender, like a love-hate relationship, goes on between Peter and the pastor. Both of them are streetwise, and each respects the other's sharpness, but they still get mad at each other. The pastor hates to see Peter play the religious hypocrite, making a great show of saying the Rosary in front of the tabernacle when he sees he has an audience.

Recently, Peter was angry with the pastor for throwing him out of church. Peter complained: "I got held up on my way to Mass, and the police came." The pastor, not trusting Peter's story, asked him to leave. At one o'clock the next morning, Peter (flanked by two buddies in front of the church) registered an oath with me that he was going to get even with the pastor by kicking his Irish behind. Peter felt brave, because he knew the pastor was asleep. I decided not to tell the pastor about the threat. They are old enough to skirmish without help from me.

Peter is smarter than the average street person, and is probably highly educated, if you can believe the rumors. He told me: "I'm a bilingual panhandler. I can do it in German and Spanish." He is also a sharp judge of human nature. He saw me with some people whom he hustled for money, but they ignored him. Later, he said: "You have very cheap friends."

He only takes money from me when he's hungry, or saving up for a rosary. If he wants to buy pot, he won't take a dime, openly telling me he's getting money for marijuana. He goes through three or four rosaries a week. "Somebody steals them," he complains. White plastic beads, conspicuously exhibited, are part of his appeal, though I don't question whether he is religiously sincere.

Peter, with his begging, is no more dishonest than the rest of us. He keeps us humble with his frankness. I would trust him more than I trust the clerics who go poor-mouthing to widows. In these neighborhoods, you keep an eye on the local characters, hoping that if you need them they will be keeping an eye on you.

Another fellow makes a habit of sitting on the stoop of the deli next door. He always has a pen and paper in his hands as though writing a letter. He reminds me of my brother. My brother, as a young man, used to go away on unannounced trips. He'd send letters home so my parents wouldn't worry. I will always remember these letters: plain and simple, yet painstakingly written so that they made the sender seem vulnerable. Only sailors, wayfarers, guys down on their luck or out of work, prisoners, or boys away from home write such letters, using some flat surface propped against their knees as a desk, with the words close together to save space. Yet they never have enough to say to fill out the page.

Every time I see this chap who reminds me of my brother, I want to ask him if he needs money. He never looks at me, because he is busy with his pen. Lately, I've stopped imagining that he is letter-writing. Either he is an artist making drawings, or he is an anarchist drawing up manifestos. He still keeps the sweet, pitiable appearance of the older brother I never got close to as a kid. It makes me feel like crying to look at him.

Coming through Washington Square Park, I got

splashed by a dog on a leash that was being walked too close to the sidewalk. I was on my way to dinner, and had to go home and change. It was a nuisance, but I stayed good-natured. It wasn't the dog's fault if I got humiliated by a freak accident. New York has never done me any real harm. Walking the streets late at night, I've always felt safe. At the rectory, I saw in the papers they want to canonize the late Cardinal Cooke. It seems like a mistake. He was a fine man who died like a hero, but it's too soon to turn his life into a cause, trying to give the people a saint they haven't asked for. Too much else is going on to bother with a canonization they shouldn't have time for.

In Times Square, members of a black church meet on a street corner, squeezing hymns out of a harmonium, and offering free redemption. I'm sure God makes use of them, but it always surprises me to see evangelists competing for attention with pimps and hustlers. Does Christ seated in glory need this kind of huckstering, with His mercy showcased like the cheap neckties the vendors have arranged on a pushcart? I can't insist that God in His humility needs a cathedral to show off His love. Wanting to draw men into the circle of His love, He turns everything into grace.

I listen to the old-time religion, thinking cynically how inadequate it sounds to me. God went to the trouble of making Adam and Eve, and the devil upstaged Him with a successful temptation. Ever since, there has been warfare between heaven and hell, with God trying to get His creatures back from Satan's power. Despite the efforts of Christ, many people — unless there's a drastic change in them — will be damned as sinners in a lake of fire. In terms of the head count, the archenemy is the big winner; starting with nothing, he takes most of mankind to be imprisoned with him in hell. God's purpose in creation seems seriously frustrated by a spoiled angel He threw out of glory. God sounds like a stable-master who keeps locking the barn doors after the horses are gone.

I prefer to believe that God is in charge of history as He was in charge of evolution, turning apparent defeats into pathways of His will. Theology, when you think of it, is a regular Noah's ark of differing opinions. The preacher says: "I read my Bible, and I'm going to heaven. You're a Catholic, doing Catholic things like going to Communion and praying to Mary, which will not save you, so Satan is your father." In my Father's house, there are many mansions. One narrow-minded man wraps himself in the exegesis of Scriptures which he only dimly understands, and poses in public as a prophet. Certain Catholics are just as limited, bullying priests with dire predictions from highly questionable visions of God's Mother warning Americans about the consequences of their sins.

It seems to me a question of empowerment: By whose authority do you teach these things? The Pentecostals claim the Holy Spirit; the social justice evangelist claims the great judgment scene in Matthew 10:42 ("Whoever gives a cup of cold water to one of these lowly ones . . ."). As a priest, I claim the guidance of the Catholic Church, witness of the life of Jesus, Lamb of God and Savior of the world — the powerhouse of grace through which God enters our lives, and brings us in touch with His life. All of us professing Christ as Lord are members, perfectly or imperfectly, of the Body of Christ. Each of us has some claim to the truth, provided we are not caricaturing the Gospel with sheer hatred. There are many different styles of being Christian. The Quakers have a style. The Episcopalians have several styles rang-ing from high church to low church. Fundamentalists have a style which can make them sound righteous, but you shouldn't let them fool you with their kind of simplistic zeal. To an outsider, it must sound as though all of us were playing the Abbott and Costello game of "Who's on first?"

It doesn't make sense, pitting *us* against *them*, saved against lost, orthodox versus heretic, Catholic against Protestant. Whether we like it or not, we Christians are a mixed bag featuring such assorted types as Dorothy Day, Bishop Pike, Jimmy Swaggart, the Blue Army, Daniel Berrigan; the charismatics, the born-agains, the Jews for Jesus, the snake handlers; the Yale Divinity School, the National Council of Churches, and the nameless religious flakes who embarrass the name of denominational religion from coast to coast. Maybe, without knowing it, we are co-conspirators with the Communist Party and the atheistic humanists. God, wanting to build His kingdom, turns everything into grace. Everything having truth and goodness in it is useful to grace. The Communist Party, when it has a passion for caring for the sufferings of mankind, could become a ministry of grace, though one doesn't forget the purges of Stalin. We had no way of breaking into God's world, so He broke into our world; and, like the Christ of history, He doesn't mind the company He keeps.

It's given me much pleasure reading theologians like Rahner, whose vision is broad and whose faith is deep. Yet, as I grow close to the age of sixty, I'm safer close to the tradition. Older men, grown liberal, are apt to sound wishy-washy. But Rahner's views seem as traditional as Bernanos's country priest, who sums up Rahner, as I understand him, when he says: "Grace is everywhere."

That is why, in writing this, I examine trivia. That is

why I enjoy walking the sidewalks of New York looking for evidence, in the ordinary lives of people, of a ubiquitous grace at work and play, bringing us home to heaven.

CHAPTER 7

A
Delicate
Bondage

I've often noticed the regularity with which births follow deaths in families where members have died. When my grandparents (on my father's side) died at Thanksgiving time many years ago, before the following September my sister had a baby, and my cousin had a baby. When my father died three years later, my sister had a second child, born within the year.

The timetables of births and deaths never seemed planned by any conscious arrangement that families have made. Heaven has a way of giving, and of taking away, keeping the silence about its intentions. An ancient rumor tells of God's keeping watch at the fall of sparrows; one supposes He comforts the grief of our losses with the joy of the new lives we gain. Babies don't serve as substitutes for the loved ones who die; they create a space for themselves that was never there before. They help our hearts find new ways of being useful. They keep the world young enough to be wise in not attempting to hold on to the old.

It is sweet to watch a couple becoming parents for the first time. Some women are never lovelier than when they are harboring a new life in the personal accommodations which pregnancy requires. Michele (who was pregnant when I wrote this) was beautiful, and she knew she was beautiful, and Bill was proud of a wife whom strangers smiled to see, out of pleasure at meeting a woman blessed.

At lunch, one day, I asked them questions so that they could tell me what it was like. As the priest who married them, I felt I had a right to know the personal details which were not too private for sharing. Michele spoke of the morning sickness at the beginning, which made her wonder why a woman would bother to have more than one child. Now, she said, she was certain that she would not settle for less than a dozen.

"At night," she said, "I can feel the baby kicking." The kicking might indicate, I pointed out, that if the baby was a boy, he would be a football player; or, if a girl, she might become a Rockette.

The work of creation — in the space under Michele's heart — went on quietly enough as we lunched. (Michele said the space under her heart was where the baby was, though sometimes it shifted around.) I thought of cables being stitched, attaching muscles to the brain, and a soul wedding itself to flesh, incarnating itself in tiny fists and feet. If those feet kicked their heels in a prenatal dance, Michele never mentioned the commotion.

I'd never insist that couples have large numbers of children. A baby is not to blame because it lives so dependently for so long a time. I have raised dogs from puppyhood. You can't ignore a puppy; you can't leave him alone for long periods without something happening; and if you hear him whimpering in the night, you know he needs to be helped. Yet, by instinct, he learns to drink water from whatever spot he finds wet, even the fish tank, if he thinks it necessary; or he can find food to feed himself, if you should forget, by which he can survive. A puppy needs company for his training and his sense of well-being and security. If he's young enough, you can fool him for a while with the ticking of a clock, if the clock is wrapped in a sweater.

But babies, as I observe them from the rectory, are absolutely helpless. All the instruments are in place, finely tuned for use, as age brings experience. A parent looks at little fingers, perfectly formed; and the dreams begin of some future cleverness deserving of praise for hands that can mend a brain or write a sonata for the piano.

In the meantime, for many years of life, parents are in bondage day and night. If the parents are hungry, the child's meal must come first; if they are weary, they must postpone their rest until an urchin's eyes are closed in slumber. If the baby is sick — perhaps suffering from colic or from a throbbing pain along the gum line of an uncut tooth — the child must be attended to before parents can allow themselves the luxury of a terminal headache. You can't say to a baby: "Fair is fair; you've had your fun, now let me have mine." As far as a baby is concerned, that's not the way the contract is written.

Of all love, having a baby is the tenderest love. Babies do sometimes smile, or gurgle an affection, or act beguilingly precocious, supportive of a hope that you've fielded a thoroughbred. As a bachelor who loves children, I've always known that courage is needed to take the risk of an unconditional attachment to an untested stranger, who guarantees nothing on his arrival but his need for attention. Wanting a baby seems like a moral miracle, more wonderful than the chemistry of elements that spin themselves out into the mystery of bone and blood.

Bill said: "We are hoping that you will give us the honor of your doing the baptism."

"How lovely to be asked," I said. "I would be thrilled."

Baptism represents a decision to do everything over again, on a higher level: the begetting and birth, the naming, the new identity and genealogy in the family of God, the new set of parents whose duty it is to watch the soul. The rituals enacted with thumb and fingers on a baby's head seem like an exaltation of the ordinary; there's not much here the infant hasn't experienced before: a splashing with water; anointing with oil, dabbed off with cotton; the gift of a robe and a candle; the murmuring of promises in an urchin's ear. Sacraments have all the elements of everyday life; yet there is a solemnity of intentions to them that represents heaven.

We ate sherbert as I thought of sacraments bearing life from the cross.

Michele said: "You know, having a baby changes you. Before, we thought of ourselves as a couple of young professionals making their way in the world. We were close, yet we seemed to lead separate existences. Now, we think how close we are, and how the baby keeps bringing us closer. . . ."

"She's becoming more affectionate," Bill said. "We've gotten much nearer our families."

An hour before, at Mass, I had read them a verse of Scripture from John: "I solemnly assure you, / unless the grain of wheat falls to the earth and dies, / it remains just a grain of wheat. / But if it dies, / it produces much fruit" (12:24).

Our Lord was speaking a truth familiar, I suppose, to farmers; but he was also using a metaphor that should be helpful to a priest. In sacraments, I could describe the paradoxes of life from death; but how does it work in having a baby, this cycle of death preceding birth, this dying before new life comes?

Michele and Bill wouldn't have known. I might have frightened them if I had asked.

But they had given me a clue. They seemed to be telling me that some old way of life was being left behind them, some sense of self-centeredness outgrown, as they felt their personal love being drawn into a partnership with God's love in the birth of a child.

Michele said: "I think the baby liked the sherbert. I can feel him stirring." If I had wanted, she would have let me touch her stomach to feel the movement. But my hands were too shy. I put them under the table, out of harm's way. It would have been nice, but I felt I should wait awhile, before making the baby's acquaintance.

The Most Welcome Guest At The Wedding

Before you ever read the books, or talked with your parents, or were warned by the priest, you knew about sex. You heard jokes about sex in the school yard. You used dirty words before you understood what they meant. Growing up, you thought of sex as something older kids did. You knew they were wrong — that they should be ashamed of themselves; it was undoubtedly a sin, but they did it anyway. The fellows who did it were daredevils; the girls who did it were cheap. God help the guy who made smart cracks about your sister. God help your sister, if she did anything that looked or sounded cheap.

117

In high school, several girls who got pregnant, leaving school in the middle of the year, were classmates you had known since grade school. Any girl who moved away was suspected of going to some grim home to have a baby. Your parents said many times that they trusted you. Their trust was a warning not to let your sexuality lead you into trouble.

Babies, you learned, could be a problem even for married people. A high-school chum told me of his parents' attempts to deal with his mother's unwanted pregnancy. The woman was thirty-five; she already had a large family. Both parents had promised the other there would be no more children, even if it meant birth control, which they weren't crazy about, because, as Catholics, they would have trouble with the priest.

His mother's discovery of her condition was one of the discouraging things that happened to a woman weary with childbearing; only the news of breast cancer could seem more threatening. What, the frantic parents asked each other, were they going to do?

On a Saturday evening, the husband, the wife, and the wife's sister sat down at the kitchen table with a fifth of whiskey and a single glass. Their hope was to get the pregnant woman violently sick on booze so that the resulting nausea and vomiting might lead to a miscarriage. The other children, living closely as a big family in a small house, knew what was happening without being told. Their mother, drinking joylessly and efficiently, held her liquor like a trooper. When she had drunk enough she fell asleep. Her efforts at a miscarriage had earned her a good night's sleep.

When you were growing up, the consequences of sexuality were always there to threaten you, the unrivaled facts of life. A girl could get pregnant at a Sunday school picnic or at the junior prom, if someone sneaked in liquor. Some fellows, wanting to be big shots, carried contraceptives in their wallets. Carried long enough, those contraceptives, from their disuse, became negative symbols of innocence. Fear and common sense kept most kids chaste, in their bodies, if not in their imaginations.

A bit of common sense, part of folk wisdom, belonged among the self-evident truths of adolescence: getting a girl pregnant was plenty of trouble. Pregnancies could happen, if you fooled around. All of us knew examples. I grew up with a decent bunch of kids, many of them religiously and morally motivated. Those who played the sexual games were only a little less innocent than the rest of us. They were just more reckless in taking chances. Preferring passion to prudence, they got into trouble.

Before you learn a philosophy or theology, you pick up tips from observing life. Somewhere, there is a tasteless little card that says it all: it shows a character from the funny papers, unexpectedly pregnant. The character sums up her chagrin in a rueful caption: "I should have danced all night." Because she didn't dance all night, she had a problem. An eleventh commandment warns: "Thou shalt not get caught." Pregnancy, to people of my generation, meant that you had been caught at something. You really wished you had decided to dance all night.

Every generation has parents that dread a birth. In ghettoes, in South American jungles, on college campuses, in affuent homes, in the slums, the cry goes up: "We don't want the child." Death, sickness, love, sex, birth: they go on in worlds that never heard of Christ, along with fear, dread, anxiety, passion, lust, fulfillment. These are the moods of the human condition. Grace builds on nature, the scholastics say; where do you begin the healing?

I am one of those who worry about an age that has lost its reverence for life. The arguments — legal, ethical, moral, medical — go back and forth, pro and con, on the moment of fusion between physical elements and immortal stirrings. I grow cynical at what people believe about the sacredness of life. I've met too many couples who fear babies as though they were garlands of albatrosses being hung around their parents' necks.

A couple comes to talk. They are nervous and embarrassed with the priest. She is pregnant, and they've decided on an abortion. Nevertheless, they want to hear the Church's view. They'll give the priest his chance. I am invited to stir up their Catholic faith.

"It would kill our parents," the young man says. He doesn't know it, but once a priest had the same kind of talk with his parents (who were unmarried at the time) when he, the young man, was in the womb. His parents had felt that news of his coming would kill *their* parents.

"In all my experience," I tell them, "I've never known grandparents who didn't survive childbirth."

Recently, I told a priest-friend how beautiful I felt the vision of the Church to be. Ten years ago, the peaceniks of the Vietnam era seemed to be the true prophets of peace. The Church, in its hierarchy, looked as though it were lacking in prophets: there were just tired old popes and jingoistic bishops. Nowadays, I said, the antiwar rhetoric against Vietnam seems curiously dated, the promotional rhetoric of an *ad hoc* cause. The pope, on the other hand, speaks for the ages; again and again, I find eternity in his words. John Paul II has a greatness, along with Paul VI, that will survive the passage of time. The two men are beginning to emerge as authentic and heroic witnesses to the truth of God. They have grown in importance, and their critics have shrunk.

After years of worry, I said, I'm even feeling relieved about the Catholic thinking on birth control. Scholars said that on this great issue, the Church missed the boat, and became an irrelevance. In times when couples suffer from "the contraceptive mentality" — an unwillingness to have children — wisdom needs a voice that insists on the importance of family life. The Church is in business to remind people that true fulfillment, on earth as in heaven, lies in an extraordinary openness to the possibilities of life.

My priest-friend asked: "How do you pass this on to young people?"

"Maybe I can't pass it on," I said. "It took more than fifty years to learn it myself."

A young woman, planning her marriage ceremony, announced her unwillingness to accept children lovingly from God. She wanted the priest to omit that part from the service. "The Church is making me promise, if I get pregnant, not to have an abortion."

"The Church takes it for granted you won't have an abortion," I said. "But you are not free to deliberately exclude from your marriage the possibility of offspring."

"I won't make any promise to the Church about having children," she said. "I'll not promise never to have an abortion."

"Honey," I said, "you and I have got to have a talk." I must try to build a bridge from her life to the faith of the Church. Birth, like death, changes a safe, familiar world. I must talk down her fears and ambitions, showing her, if I can, how love and loveliness grow rich on life. Neither the Church, with its documents, nor the state, with its laws, can adequately state the case for the ways in which children are wonderful. A priest can do it, if he's lucky; parents can do it; friends can do it. Children have always been wonderful, I think, even when they are born to unmarried teenagers, if my generation in its salad days had been wise enough to know it. Sam and Janet were getting married. The priest suggested a modest wedding because the bride's condition was obvious. Sam and Janet said: "We're not trying to hide anything. We're proud of the pregnancy. If we didn't want it, we know what to do. Our baby will be the most welcome guest at his parents' wedding."

The priest thought: It's not traditional morality; but in the age of the pill and the clinics, it sounds pretty healthy.

In Eliot's *The Waste Land*, nothing grows, death overshadows life, and the land is barren. Lil, choosing to be as unfruitful as the earth, has ruined herself with pills to bring off an abortion. The wasteland waiting for rain is an image of a society needing God's grace. All my life, I've seen the wasteland coming. The world seems half in love with irresponsible death.

It startles me to see Sam and Janet, with her five months pregnant, come down the aisle as bride and groom. I sanctify the union for the sake of impending parenthood and the most welcome guest. The wasteland needs this marriage as a sign. Innocence will have a broader definition because Sam and Janet were not ashamed or afraid to have their child.

With a happiness like old Simeon's, I welcome the child to the Temple. The holy water blessing the marriage bond, I think, is a foreshadowing of the baptism washing away original sin. The Lord says: "Let the children come to me. Do not hinder them. The kingdom of God belongs to such as these" (Matthew 19:14).

CHAPTER 8

Mr. Franklin's Idea Of Heaven

Going out early for coffee, I met old Eliza, paranoid with guilt from ancient offenses, fearful of God as though He were a supermarket security guard watching her and waiting to catch her in the act of shoplifting.

"Oh," she said, "you're back." She was pleased to see me, immediately planning a talk, for the peace of her conscience. I hugged her as an old friend. I would have kissed her too; but if I had, I knew that, eventually, she would ask: "Is it a sin if a priest kisses you?" She wouldn't have been able to accept such familiarity without guilt, especially if she enjoyed it.

She said: "A priest told me in confession that the only mortal sin is putting God out of your life. I've gotten a lot of comfort from that."

"That's good, Eliza," I said. "That's the exact truth."

"Does that mean," she said, "that if I miss Mass on Sunday, it isn't a mortal sin?"

I hesitated to say yes or no. Who wants to deal with scrupulosity before morning coffee? Instead I replied, "Oh, my dear, if you missed Mass, it would surely be from sickness or weariness. I don't think God would count it against you as a serious sin. It would hardly amount to putting Him out of your life."

"So missing Mass isn't a mortal sin?"

"Don't worry about it," I said. I didn't have the energy or courage to get on the carousel of her hypothetical questions. She feared God, but she didn't trust Him. She might have enjoyed life more if she *had* put Him out of her life. I accept the responsibility of telling her not to worry. "He keeps you in His grace, Eliza," I said. "We would both know if you had given up His grace."

Later, I saw the police ambulance in front of an old brownstone. They were bringing out a body, wrapped in a blanket. "He killed himself," an onlooker explained. "He hung himself in the bathroom."

"Why?" someone asked.

"In these neighborhoods, who can tell?" an old man answered. "He was only twenty-two years old." The old man was obviously angry at such a waste of life. I offered the departed soul a conditional absolution as the ambulance pulled away.

In the afternoon, an emotional Eliza asked to speak with me in the rectory office. On seeing me, she put her hand on my arm as she said, "David was my neighbor's boy. He went to college. This morning, he did away with himself."

"On Barrow Street?" I asked. She nodded. In New York, the anonymous stranger is more identifiable in his death than in his life. Eliza fixed wet, worried eyes on my eyes. "Is killing yourself a mortal sin?" she said. She wanted an assurance that the young man had died in the friendship of God.

"Oh, Eliza," I said. "You knew him. What do you think?"

"He was Jewish," she said. "He went to college. He was my neighbor's boy. She found him dead when she came back from the deli. He did it to himself." I shook my head at the sadness.

"What will God do with him?" she said. "If his mother asks, what shall I tell her the priest said?"

"Eliza, I don't even know the man," I replied. I grew nervous, thinking of her offering comfort in my name. She was not a woman you would send on delicate errands. I couldn't imagine a Jewish mother needing her as a Catholic spokesperson on suicide, neither now, when the grief was fresh, nor later, if the death became a subject of conversation among neighbors.

"He laid violent hands on himself," Eliza said. "That's one of the worst sins of all." The poor soul sat there with tears streaming down her cheeks. She is grieving, I thought, for the death of a soul.

She was old, and in ways very childlike, but you could never talk her out of her fear of the devil, waiting for her slightest infidelity to virtue, to snatch away her soul to hell. She needed reassurance about forgiveness for all the imaginable sins, her own and everyone else's. It seemed wise, when, in her imagination, she was trying on the forms of wickedness for size, to try to make her laugh at her own foolishness. Now David, whom she knew, had made a dark, terrible decision. Laughter was not possible at David's death. How could I excuse him in her eyes for an irreversible act?

"Do you know why it happened?" I asked. "Had he been sick? Was he on drugs? Did he have a girlfriend?" I sounded to myself like a policeman. A detective would search for the motives a person had for cashing in the chips. Locating the pain that darkens the mind and twists the will into self-hatred only takes you a little way into the despair that desires dying. Survivors, wondering if things could have turned out differently, are tormented by ambiguities and uncertainties.

Eliza, I realized quickly, hardly knew the fellow. At a time of her life when she had no close friends, he had touched her with his thoughtfulness in speaking, or doing her a kindness on the hard days of winter, so that she counted him as a dear acquaintance. Now, through his own undoing, he seemed to her doomed by the justice of God to everlasting suffering. Eliza wept for him, and for herself, for surely, she felt she was offending God by so strong a grief.

How could I help Eliza? As a priest, I felt she needed the help of a psychiatrist. A psychiatrist would probably have sent her to talk to a priest. As the priest she was talking to, I wasn't prepared to lead her on a long journey into the mystery of God's will.

"Eliza," I said after a moment of silence, "how would you like to have some ice cream? Sutter's, I believe, has the best ice-cream sundaes in the whole world." Sutter's, now vanished, was a Village establishment that did tricks with milk and cream analogous to the miracles that Gucci's does with leather. Eliza, however, troubled by threats to salvation, was not some gloomy child that could be bribed into cheerfulness with an ice-cream cone. Anyway, she had her own watering places for ice cream, Haagen-Daz or Howard Johnson's. Ice cream is not a new trick you can teach old dogs.

"Well, then," I said, "how about a highball at McBell's?" A slight look of interest flickered across her eyes, before embarrassment and the old despair seemed to deepen the creases in her tired face. Overriding her protests and hesitancy, I shepherded her out the door to the next block.

"Malt does more than Milton can / To justify God's ways to man," the poet Housman says. In Eliza's case, it was a Brandy Alexander, the waitress's suggestion, and, as it turned out, an excellent suggestion indeed. It was not Eliza's habit to drink, but the Brandy Alexander went down as easily as her mother's milk. Then I suggested a ham sandwich and a cup of coffee as a *ne noceat potus*, but Eliza preferred pastrami. Then she had a drink for the road, and I walked her home to take a nap.

Nothing had changed for Eliza. I had helped her over a rough time, but nothing had changed. For all I knew, she might add Brandies Alexander as a new sin to her list. But for a little while, a drink and a sandwich in an Irish bar had broken the ice jam of her emotions, and we talked not as priest to penitent, but as older woman to younger man.

For those who believe, someone said about Lourdes, no explanation is necessary. For those not believing, no explanation is possible. I'm not an apologist for Brandies Alexander; I never drank one in my life.

Brandies Alexander (or, for that matter, other alcoholic drinks) are neither a miracle nor a pastoral technique. Winston Churchill once defined a fanatic as someone who won't change the subject, and can't change his mind. A hypochondriac obsessed with his health is like that. A Christian obsessed with spiritual fear is like that. Eliza, spending too much time examining her conscience, was like that. I insisted that she change the subject, telling her for a little while I would be responsible for her soul, David's soul, and the soul of the waitress serving our drinks. Liquor gave her confidence that I had the graces for the work of an archangel.

I encouraged her to conversation: of her childhood, growing up in Brooklyn; her years going to a job in Manhattan; the decades and a half she spent with a man who wouldn't marry her.

Nobody ever listened more intently than I listened to Eliza, that lonely woman who, for a long time, had had only priests to talk to, about subjects other than the weather. She tried to make herself seem important with the magnitude of her sins, so that her talks with priests became a kind of sickness that was a burden for priests to hear. The more they tried to cut her off, the more she tried to claim their attention because she knew they weren't listening, and feared they weren't understanding her.

I brought her home a bit tight, and relaxed enough to rest. Fear would be back, soon enough, to nag her. She had let go of fear for a little while; therapy or sacrament couldn't do much more. I thought what a pleasure it would be, in the case of uptight, little old ladies, to impose Brandies Alexander as a penance. "Only three, Father?" I could hear them pleading. "Couldn't you make it six, and one for the intentions of the pastor?"

"Surely, my dear," I would answer pastorally, "and I'll see if we can't get it covered by Medicare."

"Eliza," I said as I was leaving her, "do you know what Benjamin Franklin expected to happen, when he met God?" She shook her head no.

"Benjamin Franklin said that when he met the Almighty, he expected God would greet him as one Christian gentleman greets another." Eliza reflected on Mr. Franklin's idea of heaven.

"Remember that," I said, "when you start to worry about David."

"Did Benjamin Franklin also die a suicide's death?" she asked.

"No," I said, "but everyone knew he did a lot of running around." I couldn't change history, even to help Eliza.

Directions When You're Flying Blind

Agnes Sanford writes: "A resurrection took place through the service of baptism administered by my father-in-law. Summoned to baptize a dying child, he found upon his arrival the child was already dead. Whereupon he dropped the blessed water into the infant's mouth during baptism and prayed for life to return — and it did."

* * *

"Don't be mean-tempered about it," a woman once wrote me. "Don't be somebody who spoils the fun." Hers was a gentle criticism I deserved for my description of charismatic people as handclappers. I really am embarrassed by exhibitionists. The Reverend Ernest Angley, on television with Haitian children — whom he has healed of their deafness and dumbness, he claims — does not persuade me, though I would be happy for children for whom miracles happened. Humbler blessings come through the ordinary ministries, like mine. I wouldn't want to spoil the fun of the extraordinary ministers of healing.

* * *

Catholics in trouble with their faith eventually give signs of their distress. At dinner, a priest remarked that he felt God was a noninterventionist. "I've never known Him to really step in," the priest said.

"What about the sacraments?" I asked.

"Sacraments," the priest replied, "furnish the occasions on which faith becomes alive. You have no evidence that God becomes busy when a sacrament is received."

"If God never intervenes," I said, "how can you tell if He really exists?"

"Ah," said the priest, "that is the question. You can't tell if He exists."

The priest had become an agnostic. He was living out the final days of his active ministry. He was, at that time of his life, a deeply unhappy man.

* * *

"In a haunted house," my grandmother used to say, "you feel that ghosts have just left the rooms you are on the point of entering." The Holy Spirit in the world is comparatively elusive. You're always finding signs that He's been around, but He leaves it ambiguous. My grandmother said: "You're left feeling that if you were quicker, you could feel God's hand or touch His face in the darkness." My paternal grandmother was a Methodist, an evangelical famous for leaning on the Everlasting Arms, though she told me she never clapped hands. She would have enjoyed the paradox of the Catholic Eucharist, the symbolic bread and wine celebrating the nearness of Christ who is as distant as the Mansions of Glory are from wheatfields and vineyards. Grandmother would have asked: "Are Eucharists celebrated among the saints who have finished with their need for faith?"

* * *

Peter and the other fishermen were bone-tired. They had nothing to show for a night's work. They looked forward to a meal and a few hours of sleep.

The Lord greeted them as they were leaving their boats. He surprised them by telling them to let down their nets again. Peter said: "We've done the best we can. We'll keep on trying, if you think we should."

Out of respect for Jesus, they lowered the nets into

the lake. Immediately, they made the grandest catch in their lifetimes as fishermen. Peter sank to his knees, overwhelmed by the manifestation of the power in Jesus. The catch was easily explained by the skeptics in the crowd. It only takes luck, not a miracle, to catch fish in a lake full of fish.

Peter didn't argue whether Jesus was a wonder-worker, or an insightful observer of the ways of nature at sunrise. The overloaded boats were as much of a sign as Peter needed; the miracle wasn't ambiguous, because it had happened to him. On the strength of it, he left all things, even the freshly caught fish, to follow Jesus.

* * *

I wonder if Agnes Sanford's father-in-law ever had doubts. Would it occur to him to ask whether water had aroused a sleeping child? My priest-friend, turned agnostic by God's nonintervention, says that faith is a fiction belonging to the department of the imagination.

* * *

On a spring evening, I wanted to go from Boston, Massachusetts, to Portland, Maine, because my mother was sick. The trains and buses had left, so I decided to hitchhike. Making a sign reading "To Portland," I took a cab to the expressway and stood, like a young serviceman, in sight of the cars traveling north.

I was scared, because I knew I looked like a fool. After ten minutes, a car stopped. A middle-aged man asked: "Are you a Catholic priest?" I said that I was.

He said: "I'm on my way home from work, but I can take you to Portland."

On the way, he told me his life story. He was a Catholic who had given up his faith and had been away from the Church for nearly twenty-five years.

When he had finished laying his sins before me I

asked: "Would you like to make this into a sacramental confession?"

He had been waiting a long time for reconciliation. He wanted forgiveness from the Church. I gave him absolution. He said: "It seems like a miracle."

I knew nothing I could point to as a miracle, but I believed that God had certainly shaped the occasion: the priest needing a ride and resorting to hitchhiking, for the one and only time in his life; the stranger, out of touch with his Church, who was so kind, driving two hundred and fifty miles on his trip up and back; and the good confession, which made him feel blessed with pardon and peace, and left me feeling like the instrument of grace that the Lord had used.

* * *

An old professor from the campus died in circumstances that were tragic. His friends were certain he had died from grief. Everyone assumed that the professor was out of town on vacation. The body was not discovered for ten days.

One grief-stricken student became bitterly agitated over the tragedy. He could talk of nothing except the injustices surrounding the death of a good man. Finally, he was describing the professor as a sacrificial victim.

Later, when the student let go of his sorrow, he was embarrassed to remember the fervor of his emotions. "I was calling him the suffering servant of Notre Dame," he said. "That was wrong, because there is only One who can be called the Suffering Servant."

The student was a fine young Christian I was anxious to help. "There is only One who can be called the Great High Priest, but many of us share in His priesthood. Maybe we can say there are many Catholics called to be suffering servants, because they follow in the way of the

Servant of the Lord. Christ is not diminished if you recognize that the old professor, like other faithful souls at Notre Dame, had the vocation to be a suffering servant."

The words were not bad words, and they made the student feel better. The idea surprised me more than it surprised him. The helpful words come in the difficult situations when you would like to heal. In an ordinary ministry, I rely on the helpful words as gifts from God, generous with interventions.

* * *

Faith, for me, means the directions I get when I'm flying blind. Sacraments are all the promises of grace I am certified to make. All the rest of it, I play by ear. My grandmother would say I lean a lot on the Everlasting Arms. I would never clap hands with Ernest Angley, although in Haiti he plays it more by ear than I do. I would clap hands as a form of applause if I could really be sure he healed the children.

The Ministry Of Disappointment

I was buying a jacket at Gilbert's in South Bend, Indiana. The salesman, a pleasant young man, asked: "Do you know the priest who walks his dog at Notre Dame?"

Priests are a dime a dozen, but Notre Dame has only one dog, a cocker spaniel named Darby O'Gill II, and I am his roommate. I identified myself as the Oliver Hardy to my Stan Laurel of a pup, in a vaudeville act appearing daily on the campus.

"I'm getting married," the young clerk said. "My mother died last year. I would like to talk to a priest."

He told me, a complete stranger, the ordeal of his mother, physically worked over by sickness as vicious as a scavenger until, after two years, death ended her indignities. "She had faith enough to move mountains, but God never lifted a finger to save her. What good is God, if He doesn't want to help?" His eyes were swimming with wetness as he said: "Maybe I ask too many questions, but what the hell use is He if He couldn't spare my mother one moment of her pain?"

It seems better to doubt God than to curse Him. If he had not been so certain of God's existence, he would have been less angry and unforgiving.

The jacket I was buying no longer seemed important. I didn't need clothes as much as he needed healing.

* * *

Yeats, in his autobiography, describes a story he heard from Oscar Wilde during the tragic years which ended Wilde's life. The story goes something like this:

Christ meets a man, quarrelsome and brawling, picking fights with everyone he sees.

"Sir," the Lord asks, "why are you so bitter and angry with the world?"

"Lord," the man answers, "I was blind, and You gave me sight."

Jesus, continuing on His way, meets a lad so drunk that he keeps falling down.

"Young man," the Lord asks, "why have you let yourself get into this unhappy condition?"

"Lord," the fellow replies, "I was crippled, and You made me walk."

After a while, Jesus sees an old man, weeping and groaning, stretched out on a pile of refuse.

Jesus inquires: "What sorrow afflicts you that you behave so?"

The old man answers: "Lord, I was dead, and You gave me back life."

* * *

134

Old Sam, suffering from cancer, talked to me as he was dying. He kept his eyes on a crucifix opposite his bed.

Sam said: "I watch Him all the time. He could cure me with a word, if He wanted to. Why does He let me suffer?"

No answer of mine would have helped.

Sam continued: "Some priests have the healing touch. I've read about a priest who's a healer. If I could write to him, maybe he would come to the hospital."

He was asking if I was a miracle worker. My blessing was as much peace as I could give him, and I could feel his disappointment. He wanted to say: "Could you bring the priest that heals?" I couldn't even do that much for him. I don't like being a priest on the days I lose battles. Sam died six hours after I left him.

* * *

On television, I watch the preachers promising miracles. "Bring us your cancers and bodily ailments, your sins and bad habits; and in Jesus' name, BE HEALED!" Would it be worthwhile, I asked myself, to send away for their books and tapes featuring "Studies in the Word" to find out how they beat the devil at his own game?

The cameras give you glimpses of paralytics lined up in their wheelchairs, waiting to see if cures will be offered. The pope, blessing the sick, doesn't offer cures. He doesn't promise salvation to multitudes of sinners making an act of faith. The pope is modest in his claims, compared to the faith healers.

One night, a minister from Atlanta, Georgia, talked of raising his dead mother from the grave. Other evangelists, who had been successful with resurrection, would help him, he said. The poor, dear mother, kept in cold storage, waited for her great getting-up morning. One hoped that she wouldn't mind being called back and doomed again to life.

I am an imperfect Christian, wondering if it all seems like a game God is playing with His suffering children. If there is a ministry of healing, there is also a ministry of disappointment among the afflicted who also ran after the miracles. I can imagine the faces of children of a large family in a house to which the favorite uncle has brought a gift to only one lucky child. Common sense and kindness say it is not wise to play favorites. The Lord doesn't have to play fair with old Sam; His mercy is undeserved fairness. It was hard for Sam to see how the Lord tempers the wind to the shorn lamb. Human suffering is complicated enough without Sam's bitter question: "Why not me?"

A Church in which the Lord denied himself the pleasure of miracles would be very dull as the Body of Christ. Religion depends upon, and is made lovely and lively by, the unexpected favors. The hours of watching television preachers leave me with questions: the healers "claiming the promises" raise expectations so high, as though miracles should be the rule, and not the exception, among Christians born again and living in the state of grace. Is this the New Testament faith for now? Is the Church blessed by a renewal that opens the eyes of the blind? The blind may be blessed, God love them, and we wouldn't wish them in darkness, but the Gospel coming from the South seems to be disposing us to be a generation hungering and thirsting for a tent full of miracles as signs of God's love. If the dead are being physically raised, they are not being raised because of any commands to Lazarus that I am empowered to give. Have I missed the boat in a Pentecostal, charismatic age? Or is God's name — Father, Son, and Holy Spirit — a manipulative word of honey-tongued evangelists who should know better, if they are decent men? Do I also appear a charlatan, like my fellow servants of the Word, when I ask Catholics to accept the efficacy of a sacrament I am offering them as a sign of redemption, in the name of the Church which is the Bride of Christ?

Apostles should not be jealous, Jesus said, of magicians doing wonders, though the Apostles thought all the magic was entrusted to them. To one ministering to the disappointed, it seems that Lourdes never leaves the pilgrims bitter. Coming home still crippled, those pilgrims seem freshened by graces assuring them they are loved by heaven. Love wrapping him around was enough of a miracle to have satisfied Sam. I hope he experienced a happy death.

Lazarus laughed, they say, after his miracle, possibly because he understood that death — that fearsome passage — was a joke, like the haunted house at Disney World. Bartimaeus was certainly cured of more than his blindness; on a clear day, possibly, he could see forever. Oscar Wilde, as an emotional cripple, went home, I pray, by the way of the cross.

The only miracle I am sure of is an old-fashioned one, as I read with a Gilbert's clerk, on his way to his marriage and the Catholic faith, through the Gospel of John. Darby O'Gill II curls up at his feet, offering comfort, or finding it, in being so shaggily close. The miracle began with the young man's mother's illness. Sickbeds are like the cross, I tell him, in earning points for souls you love. His mother's love was Christ-like in enduring to the end. It's his first lesson in redemptive suffering, which is the most amazing miraculous power I am acquainted with in all the works of grace.

137

CHAPTER 9

A Willingness To Have Fathers

Becoming, and remaining, a priest, when you think of it, involves a willingness to have fathers. Neither priests nor seminarians thought much about it in my days as a student; nobody self-consciously played his role as father or son; if anything, the relationships were described under the images of brotherhood. Looking back, I recognize that the father-figures were always there; some, because they were gracious older men whom you reverenced as patriarchs; others, because you owed them obedience, affection, and respect as religious superiors.

For me, in a way, it was funny, because the most chafed-at personal bond I ever had was with my father. I once mentioned to a psychiatrist that I always felt uptight when bosses were around. The psychiatrist said: "You probably had a very strict father." Remembering my dad, a Down East Yankee, I suppose the psychiatrist was right.

My first superior was a tall,

handsome priest with silver hair, who physically resembled my biological father. To tell the truth, he terrified me. He became closer to my mother than he did to me, writing her letters to say how I was doing. He seemed concerned about me as a recent convert, and wanted my mother, two years widowed, to feel close to my seminary experience. I think her decision to be a Catholic, after I was ordained, had its beginning in my superior's kindness in writing her the news.

The superior never promised anyone that the seminary was easy. He always talked of vocation as a divine romance, which I suppose it was, if you thought of it mystically. He would always ask, as though he wanted the question to haunt us, how serious we were about our romance with God.

The truth, far from romantic, was that the seminary was a bold, ugly place. Nothing encouraged you to devotion because of its comfort or beauty. Silence was the chief rule of the house. I never knew silence was important to religion, until I began getting up in silence, going to bed in silence, and being ordered to silence on a regular schedule, so that conversations with God could begin in the quiet.

The seminary day was highly structured, with a time appointed for everything you did. The bell woke you at 6:00 A.M., and moved you from prayer to meals, to study, to recreation. (On winter mornings, the chapel windows would be kept open to discourage drowsiness.) If you ignored the bell's summons, you were breaking the Rule. The Rule, representing God's will, was more important than any private choice of your own. You measured your life to its external detail. It was not binding in sin, but it could lead to sin if you treated it flippantly. Such flippancy was interpreted to mean that you were trying to throw away your holy vocation, and what would grieve God more than that?

The final bell rang for sleep in the dormitory room you shared with nine others, all of you serious about keeping the Grand Silence of the night watch. It was blessedly sweet to steal away to the privacy of your bed.

Here in the seminary at Notre Dame, taking classes as a Notre Dame student, a lazy, comfort-loving klutz began the long journey to ordination. At the end of the first year, called the postulancy, I would be sent to the novitiate, after which, if I survived, I would take first vows as a member of the Congregation of Holy Cross.

The approval of the superior meant everything, and he wasn't an easy man to please. I felt it would have been easier if I were a natural athlete. Seminary priests like athletes best, it seems to me. I was a complete illiterate in the sports I played. We had guys who thought they could make it with the Notre Dame varsity. I ruined the games for them. I broke their hearts with disappointment, because I always got in the way.

The superior asked me which sports I played. I tried to convince him that I skated well and was a terrific swimmer. Even without seeing me perform, he knew it wasn't true. I lied a little so that he would respect me, and not feel disappointed. There's no peace in your soul when you've been dishonest with your superior.

I'm sure I exaggerated the importance of sports; but you felt that they proved you were made of the right stuff. The superior talked a lot about the Last Judgment: the Last Judgment was everlastingly important. Death was fearful because it led to the Judgment. In an early talk, he announced that his very next Mass, on the following morning, would be offered for the seminarian among us who died first. The superior said he didn't know, and we didn't know who the fellow was, but God knew his name. Any fellow facing the Last Judgment would need all the graces he could get. The superior's words made us shiver, although they represented a general warning, with nothing personal intended. One of the seminarians drowned the following summer. He had dropped out of the program at the end of the year, because he couldn't feel serious about keeping the Rule. We all knew who got the graces from the superior's Mass.

Manners, the superior told us, were also important. More souls had been lost, he said as he chewed a toothpick, by bad manners in priests than by bad morals in priests. As an example of style, he showed us how to break rolls, piece by piece, buttering every couple of mouthfuls as we went.

I was warned that the superior was concerned about my lack of community spirit. This meant I avoided recreation periods as often as I could, either finding excuses to study, or not bothering to show up. However good my reasons, I was told, missing recreation was against the Rule. I was not a good mixer. Religious communities do not encourage members to be lone wolves.

At the end of the year, the superior told me he wasn't sending me to the novitiate. I wasn't ready, he said. He wanted to keep me as a postulant for another year, continuing with my classes at Notre Dame. I was too recent a convert, he felt. Other fellows had imbibed faith with their mother's milk; Catholicism had been passed down in their families for years.

I tried to argue with him, to convince him that I was as ready as anyone. I could hear myself slurring words as I talked, because I was so afraid of what he was saying. I think now that the fear I brought him to deal with was a form of love. I tried explaining my clumsiness at games, and how I had done the best I could to be sociable. I couldn't explain anything except with truth that sounded like a lie even to me.

He let me babble, waiting, I think, to hear a more eloquent side of me. Keeping quiet, I figured, with this stern man representing the priesthood and the Church would get me nothing but disappointment in the vocation I had set my heart on.

Finally, he stopped me. "Some fellows go through hell and high water to become priests," he said. "Some of them here have seen rough times in the war. They have the toughness to survive. What about your toughness? How badly do you want to become a priest?"

I've wondered what my father would have thought of this Catholic priest. My dad felt I had let him down when I became a Catholic; he also thought the decision was childish. His grief came through to me as gruffness, and I was afraid of him. Now here was my superior speaking sternly. I think my father would have applauded his playing tough.

The other seminarians got measured for the habits they would wear as novices. I had to explain my unreadiness because of my descent from Protestant stock. I hated the look in their eyes that said they were sorry.

In September, I began my second year as a postulant, alongside of guys presumed to be secure in their faith because they had fought in the war and were lifelong Catholics. Again, I was held accountable for my actions in a world made cheerless by rules and bells.

In April, my superior allowed me to go through the prescribed ritual of petitioning, on my knees, for entrance into the novitiate. He looked at me over his glasses, invited me to sit down, and began grinning like Tom Sawyer caught at mischief. The smile was boyish on the face of that giant man with the silver hair. I could see laughter in his eyes, kindness in his manner. I understood he had been on my side the whole dumb time.

"I think you're going to make it," he said. "Use your head, and don't wear yourself out with emotional binges." Then, sticking out his hand, he said: "Get measured for a habit at the tailor shop. Good luck, and enjoy the novitiate."

He was my first father in faith in the Holy Cross community. Others came later, but none ever seemed to hide so much love under so much severity. I could have hated the vow of obedience, because it's still not easy to explain my mistakes. My dad, talking to me about a problem I was going through as a little boy, said: "I'm trying to help you, if you'll only let me." A child's best wisdom is in understanding and accepting the ways a parent can help.

The Crippled Man
Will Dance With Joy

A one-legged man came into the sacristy after Mass, asking for help. "Some people are trying to crucify me," he said.

"You get that feeling too?" I asked. I thought of Pierre Teilhard de Chardin's reaction on seeing the great Dominican Reginald Garrigou-Lagrange at a party in Rome. "There goes the man who would like to see me burned at the stake," said Teilhard. On hearing the story, one doesn't know if it was the Dominican or the Jesuit who needed watching.

There is a professional unpleasantness called *odium theologicum* that exists between rival theologians; a hatred that zealots bear toward those they perceive to be teachers of false doctrine, graceless enough to be considered God's enemies. On the other hand, there is old-fashioned paranoia. If Teilhard had brought his complaint to me, I might have sent him to the outpatient clinic at St. Vincent's to see if the doctors felt he had a leg to stand on.

Meanwhile, in the Village, a strange little man on crutches tells me of enemies out to destroy him and his family. "I thought they would be satisfied with just my leg," he said. "Now, they want all of us."

It seemed like selfishness to want all of them. I could have told him when they are out to get you, your legs are just the beginning, but it didn't seem cheerful. "How did you lose your leg?" I asked.

"I stepped on some rusty nails," he said. "My father and mother were fighting and I ran away. I hid in a place where there were boards with nails in them." He took my hand. "I've tried so hard to be God's child," he said. "Now I want to stay here with you."

"God will take care of you," I said helplessly. It's a clerical cop-out, when you don't know what to do, to lay the responsibility on God. "The ladies of the Rosary Society are in the church saying their prayers," I added. "Go out there and ask them to pray for you. Prayers protect you better than anything against nails."

"Can I have some water?" he asked. It seemed like the enactment of a Gospel truth to give a thirsty man water. He had to drink from the faucet, because I had neither cup nor glass to serve him with. He went about it like a drought-ridden camel. Then, without a further word between us, he left the safety of the sacristy to return to Sixth Avenue where, eventually, as he expects, he may find Calvary.

The city in the summer is full of tragedy and comedy. One Saturday evening a wizened old character, whose face seemed carved out of roots, asked to see a priest because his Social Security check hadn't come. Could I give him money to get his clothes from the cleaner's for church tomorrow? I gave him a buck, certain there was not a rag he owned that had ever visited the cleaner's. He was pleased with what he got, and I was happy to buy off my conscience with a dollar.

Street musicians along the sidewalk give concerts in the evening: fife and bagpipe; brass quintets from Juilliard; a woman who sings, perhaps more aptly described as a ghost that parodies prettiness. Her voice is now a screech, her once elegant dress is none too clean, her beauty is faded; an old show girl, down on her luck, singing Puccini to a taped piano accompaniment, at the corner of Christopher and Seventh Avenue.

A crowd listens to her extraordinary performance, not sure whether to take her seriously. They leave money in a tin cup as an encouragement to the curbside Galli-Curci. Farther uptown, a Louis Armstrong figure sits on a soapbox, saxophone placed to his lips, on which not a note is sounded. His hat is on the sidewalk in front of him in hope of money; not for a performance, but the pantomime of a performance, given in the expectation that shadow will be accepted as substance. Nearby, two blacks put on a show: one doing a soft-shoe, the other playing a tune on a comb — not with tissue, but just humming through the naked teeth of a comb that has seen better days.

In the park, a man walks by with clumsy gait, as though one foot was trying to find out what the other foot was doing. The beaten shoes looked half empty, and I wondered if he had lost his toes. I watched him sit down on another bench, remove his shoes, and air the bare stumps which had undergone amputation almost to the ankle. He must have stepped into a lawnmower, I thought, or lost half of each foot in an operation after frostbite.

The nuns, attending their vegetable patch, complain of the squirrels coming from Washington Square to eat their tomatoes. I'm fond of the nuns, but I'm rooting for the squirrels. Who could believe their magnificence in surviving the concrete jungle? On Forty-second Street, kids desperate for money intimidate the tourists. Approaching cars stalled in traffic, they make an offer: "Wash your windows, mister?" For those who refuse, they carry sticks with large nails in them, leaving scratches on the side of the car. Some kids earn a hundred dollars a day, with no tax deductions.

On bad days, anyone can feel like a victim awaiting crucifixion. On such days it helps to remember the mystery of suffering, from which the grace of the sacraments comes; the terror and horror which is summed up so dispassionately in the Apostles' Creed. Catholics love the liturgy, whether in Latin or in English, in which God is present under forms of bread and wine: His Eucharist, lying on our snow-white linens, while our altars are lighted from the purest wax of the industrious bee. In terse Greek metaphysics, we sum up our faith, and we're proud to sing the praises of the "Gloria."

Religious language is often metaphysical. Old women, wrapped in newspapers, asleep in doorways, aren't the least metaphysical. Where do you place them in a Christian's creed? Old men drunk in the park are also part of a liturgy, though they lack an innocence that conforms them to Christ. You can imagine the broken body of God taken down from the cross. Who would have thought it possible, out of the mess of broken flesh and blood, for Catholics, remembering the Last Supper, to make rituals out of pain?

Pope John Paul II was endearing and unforgettable in England as he administered the sacrament of healing to the sick. Nothing he could have said or done would have been more Christ-like or beautiful. One is grateful for the memory of the pope in touch with the troubles of the world.

In the midst of a society familiar with heartbreak, *odium theologicum* is alive and well, from what I read in the papers. There is something wrong in zeal that has so much anger; something missing in zeal that is more fearful than loving. A priest has recently written how difficult he would find it to put his heart into a sermon on vocations. "Most of us would be very slow to encourage a really pious young person to be a priest or nun today. We wouldn't want to be responsible for their losing the Catholic faith."

Here, I think, is also a man who suffers from a sense of an essential loss: a mutilated Church seems more tragic than a mutilated limb. With an ordination dating back to 1954, I know what he is saying. Sometimes, comparing myself to the young fellows offering Mass, I feel like a dinosaur. I am who I am, and nothing can change it. I am a pre-Vatican II priest who studied Noldin for morals and Herve for dogma, with a preference for Wapelhorst over Fortescue in matters of liturgy, though I've read Raymond Brown in Scripture, and most of Schillebeeckx, whom I find impressive but taxing. I refuse to be written off as an anachronism. Faith is always a flickering candle, but I trust God to protect the flame from the winds that would blow it out.

Despite letters from critics who find me theologically odious, I believe with all my soul in creeds and hierarchy. I believe in priests, young and old, liberal and conservative, Democrats and Republicans. I believe, no doubt sentimentally, in the anointed hands of priests, and in the work the Church has given those anointed hands to do. I believe in candles burning at the tabernacle, signifying the presence of the Lord in the Eucharist. I believe in the Holy Spirit, the Sacred Heart, and the Blessed Virgin Mary. I share dogmas with Teresa of Ávila, John Henry Newman, Gerard Manley Hopkins, and the Curé of Ars. I believe in the Baltimore Catechism, the Ten Commandments, the Precepts of the Church, including the obligation to support my pastor in the style to which he is accustomed. I would also believe in the *Syllabus of Errors*, if I thought the pope required it, or in the importance of the Papal States to the mission of the See of Peter, if it were still proximate to heresy, as it once was, to believe otherwise. I believe in the encyclicals and councils, from Jerusalem to Vatican II. I am, however, a little shaky on some of the reports from Lourdes and Fatima. I have said and done some *dumb things*, which I regret now. By God's holy grace, I believe in the Catholic faith, whole and entire.

I also believe that the crippled man will dance with joy in heaven; and that old winos, with their innocence restored, will crowd with the children into the presence of the Redeemer like the youngest saints in the kingdom. I believe that Garrigou-Lagrange and Teilhard de Chardin will take in each other's wings and haloes for laundering, as a token sign of mutual admiration.

With such Christian optimism, based on the hope flowing from the New Testament promises and the bodily resurrection of Jesus, wouldn't it be a mistake to discourage pious young people, and the daredevils as well, from becoming nuns and priests?

I hope the parish ladies, who say the Rosary, will pray for vocations to the Church.

"I could write plays as fine as the plays of Shakespeare, if I had a mind to," said the poet Wordsworth to Coleridge.

"Obviously all that is lacking is the mind," said Coleridge, like a Charles Lamb without guile.

With priests who give up, it is the heart that is lacking, not the mind. "I haven't got the heart for it," says the discouraged Christian. Without the heart, the eyes are deceived by the evidence that is visible.

The one-legged man came back later to the church in the Village. He had decided to crucify God.

"It doesn't seem like a good idea," I said. "Why would you want to do it?"

"If someone is out to get you," he said, "shouldn't you try to get him first?"

When the mind as well as the heart is lacking, the visible evidence can look overwhelming.

The Days Of Black Chinos

The Jesuit priest giving our retreat not long ago seemed to be wearing black chino pants. I haven't seen black chinos since I was a deacon getting ready for ordination. I wouldn't know where to buy black chinos now, but black chinos and T-shirts used to be worn like uniforms under the cassocks of seminarians. Seminarians around Notre Dame have given up their cassocks except for the hand-me-downs (which sometimes scarcely cover the knees) that they wear serving feast-day Masses. Their boots and blue denim jeans call attention to themselves, as obvious as bandaged thumbs. Often, priests vested in albs are not much more formal. In 1954 how neat we all were as we were getting ready to take our places in the world as other Christs!

On this annual retreat, I started thinking of the ways I'd lived as a loner, a solitary in the midst of a community. I should have understood myself earlier; life is always harder for the lone wolf. In 1954 I tried to learn to say Mass by myself, without asking a classmate to critique me. I felt too clumsy to want to be watched. Getting the best books, I studied the rubrics, and probably spent twice as much time as the other deacons learning the gestures for a perfect Mass. It didn't work, because the old Latin Mass was very demanding; the celebrant had to be very attentive to the ways he used his hands, eyes, feet, and body. I failed the Mass test the first time, and I was afraid that they wouldn't ordain me. Some of my classmates, who had been saying Mass in their imaginations since they were schoolboys, had the professionalism of golden jubilarians. I knew the rules by heart. I needed a coach to help me translate theory into movement, and I had been too shy to ask.

Two weeks before ordination, I began using wine in my rehearsals. I wasn't used to wine, and it left me dizzy. One Saturday I appeared for lunch slightly zonked. The table, noting my hilarity, asked what I had been up to.

I said: "I've been practicing Mass, and I just trinated" — trination indicating I had done three in a row. It was such holy moments that confirmed me in a belief of Lacordaire's words: "Oh, what a life, O priest of Jesus Christ!"

One of the benefits of using Latin was that celebrants were never tempted to improve the text. A colleague bugs me with additions to the Canon, and then he personally rearranges the *Agnus Dei*: "Lamb of God, who takes away our alienation from the Father, from one another, from ourselves and You, be compassionate with us." Latin was a language none of us learned enough to tamper with. Cole Porter, hearing Sinatra stylizing "Night and Day," protested: "Sing it the way it's written, dammit." A preacher explaining the Gospel on television is always saying what the Greek text shows. The verse says that Jesus was hungry; the preacher points out that the Greek text makes it clear that He has not eaten since the day before yesterday. Common sense tells you there is no way the Greek can imply so much. The preacher finally admits that he has never studied Greek. You feel you knew it all along. Clergymen need special graces to keep them from taking liberties with God's language.

The retreat master in his conference mentions the one bread of the Eucharist. Apparently I'm the only priest alive who likes communion wafers. Catholic writers are always saying how inadequate bread is if it comes with the thinness of plastic snowflakes. My feeling about communion wafers is that they get the job done. I understand the symbolism of the nice brown loaf the parish ladies bake, but I was always touched by the thought of the religious orders of nuns who gave up their lives to make communion bread. The pale, beautiful wafers would come in boxes through the mail, more lovingly packed than Godiva chocolates selling for $19.50 a pound. Now, the flat molasses-colored discs for Sunday's Eucharist show up on the vestment case wrapped in aluminum foil; often damp to the touch because they've been made in big batches and kept in the freezer. "Thank God for the Christian Brothers," I find myself thinking. "Some year, the liturgy committee members are going to decide to stomp on the grapes themselves. Another miracle from God will be needed to turn the vinegar into wine."

I know how fragile the hosts look, and how papery they taste. But at eight o'clock Monday morning, Sunday's leftover Jesus-bread seems like the symbol of total abandonment. Soggy brown Eucharist looks like beef bits from Ken'l Ration. The Mass should be celebrated in elements that keep their dignity. Hospitality should offer a more joyful loaf to give up its substance to the sacramental presence of Christ.

Perhaps I should apologize for not liking crumbs? Some altars are always a mess; it seems that half the congregation could make their Easter duty from the leftovers on the linen. Liturgists say not to worry: the Lord at the Last Supper knew the unreliability of the accidental properties of the staff of life. Old-timers do worry. Dorothy Day worried enough to clean up the floor on her knees after Dan Berrigan's Mass. Old folks without teeth have a hard time going to Communion; they ask you with their eyes to give them something they can manage. Half the time, they leave the Lord's table looking spiritually hungry.

Traditional Catholics stick out their tongues. "Honey," I want to say, "use your hands. There's no way I can feed you like your mother on this kind of bread without something dropping." Traditional Catholics shut their eyes so they won't have to hear you.

A nun in New York does her best to guard the Eucharist against the crazies. She watches for winos approaching the chalice. On one occasion, a student of hers had to leave Mass because he was sick to his stomach. She followed him all the way home to make sure he didn't throw up the host.

This same nun told me the awful story of the kid who took Communion out of the church. He stuck the host in his pants pocket, and carried it around until it got lost, or crumbled into nothingness. Sister, catching up with the wiseacre, shook out the lint from those pockets until she was sure that the Body of the Lord had disappeared without a trace; as though, she said, the angels had taken it home. She made it sound like a rescue paralleling the resurrection.

She had the fourth-graders making holy half-hours of reparation, until the pastor stopped her. "Worse sacrileges are happening in the neighborhood," he said, meaning the prostitutes who defile their bodies, the temples of the Holy Spirit.

"God, for our sakes, becomes so vulnerable," the sister told me. "He becomes as helpless as a loose coin in a boy's overalls."

The seminarians in black chino pants would have agreed. We were ordained to be knights of the Blessed Sacrament. The hungry children, the despairing women, were not placed so directly on our consciences. Our elders knew we would find them. In 1954, they were mostly described as victims of war.

Audunsson, Sigrid Undset's master of Hestviken in thirteenth-century Norway, meditates on the only voice that spoke to him in a tongue he understood in a foreign land. ". . .The Church changed neither speech nor doctrine; she spoke to him in the holy Mass as she had spoken to him as a little boy. . . . Everywhere, when he found a church and entered it, he would be welcomed by the same voice that had spoken to him when he was a child; with open hands the Church would offer him the same sacraments that she had nourished him with in his youth. . . ."

The new theologians trace the history of pre-Vatican II sacraments to their medieval origins. The liturgy is better now, they say, because we have gone beyond the Middle Ages, to the traditions of the Fathers of the Church. The seminarians in blue denim are better informed than the deacons in black chinos were about the ways grace works.

It would be a dumb Church that wasn't smarter today than it was over thirty years ago. On annual retreat with my community, I don't regret being ordained in medievalism. All of us are equally vulnerable as a generation in Christ. We were there when they crucified Our Lord; therefore we are democrats with kings and saints. The Holy Spirit draws us together in relationships sinewed with love, and here is the miracle that surpasses liturgies. I am thirty years closer to my brothers in the Lord. Black chinos and plastic hosts tell you nothing of lifestreams in the Church.

CHAPTER 10

The Years Like Great Black Oxen

I am nearly sixty. I live in peace with my age. Physically, I see signs of the body's ruin. The face holds up, if not examined too closely; it looks its worst in the morning, when I've gone a day without shaving. Still, I can get away with knocking a year or two off my birthdays. The body is laughable; I do not feel encouraged to treat the beach crowd with the sight of me sunbathing.

It's no tragedy, being sixty. (I was born in 1925, the year *The Great Gatsby* and *The Sun Also Rises* were published. It' was a brilliant year to make one's appearance.) I've signed an uneasy armistice with ambition, passion, and disappointment. My life, so far, has turned out as well as I could have hoped for. I've had the warning signals: an early grave is possible, if I don't take care of myself. I continue to take chances: I need to avoid salt, eliminate tobacco, eat bran cereals in the morning, and jog, rather than walk, in my Adidas. Otherwise, by sixty-five, the graybeards will be saying, how young he looks to be pushing up daisies.

Three summers ago, my sister told me she was getting a reduced fare on the bus. It angered me to hear her. "No sister of mine is old enough to be counted as a senior citizen," I growled. My sister and I are in the prime of our life. My sister doesn't believe me; she is happy with the courtesies shown to seniority. When I am her age, maybe I will appreciate the reduced price of tickets to the zoo.

The "Golden Harvest," they euphemistically call it. For me, realistically, the harvesttime is not far off; for now, I'm beginning the September Song. At the Golden Harvest, they say, you realize how bountiful October can be. September is as much as I need. September still has days like summer; the season is only beginning to turn. The autumn weather will turn those leaves to flame. I've still got time for the waiting game.

Age can make you ridiculous. I am constantly repeating remembered lines from Eliot's "The Love Song of J. Alfred Prufrock":

> I grow old, I grow old;
> I shall wear the bottoms of my trousers rolled.
> Shall I part my hair behind? Do I dare to eat a peach?
> I shall wear white flannel trousers, and walk upon the
> beach.
> I hear the mermaids singing each to each . . . I fear that
> they do not sing for me.

Exactly. Prufrock tells it as it is: life can turn you into a fusty old bachelor whom the mermaids have given up on. Damn the torpedoes! Full speed ahead! Never wear rubbers in a rainstorm. Leave umbrellas at home in the wettest weather. Who needs to be that cautious, if they are singing old September's song?

The authentic hero of old age is King Lear, maddened by indignities, matching the fury of the unleashed elements with his terrible ravings, until his mind cracks; raging against the heavens that sin against him, vituperating against the thunder, until his ferocious temper, exploding again and again, burns itself out. Then with his reason returned and his strength gone, the old king, moving toward his redemption, gives a nobility to sweetness:

> Come, let's away to prison:
> We too alone will sing like birds i' the cage;
> When thou dost ask me blessing, I'll kneel down,
> And ask of thee forgiveness; so we'll live,
> And pray and sing, and tell old tales, and laugh
> At gilded butterflies. . . .

"Do not go gentle into that good night. / Rage, rage, against the dying of the light." Rage, that is, if they let you, if they don't try to make you more comfortable than you are willing to be. I remember my mother hiding medication that would help her sleep; handing the pills to me, wrapped in a Kleenex, saying she didn't want them; would I get rid of them, PLEASE! The pills were a kindness she hadn't asked for, and didn't need. Preferring to keep her faculties undimmed, she didn't want tranquilizers. There was no rage in my mother, but there was a lot of determination to see it through to the end. What good is raging, if it doesn't go anywhere, if it wears you out? Where's the sense of Dylan Thomas's poem unless you are King Lear on a stage, where redemption is possible?

Anger can be piteous, leading you to tears, with the

tears leading to anger afresh, ashamed of feeling sorry for yourself. Stanley, eighty-four, suffering from emphysema, fighting for every breath, would never count as a tragic hero. He fought and raged against the injustice of suffering until he exhausted himself to death, as a guest in a shabby room of a welfare hotel. Was he some secular Christ-figure, like Hemingway's old man of the sea, battling the odds until they defeated him, beautiful in his courage, an instructive example of grace under pressure? If so, why was he left alone to die as an irascible, unmanageable, ungrateful old grouch?

Liza, age ninety, was moved against her will to live in a hospital. She grieved every day for two years, her sorrow as fresh as sunrise, because someone, she complained, had stolen her apartment. No one — neither her children, her friends, nor the priest — would help her get her apartment back. "My things," she murmured, "where are my lovely things?" The Church has a prayer for the gift of tears. No one would ever pray to have Liza's grief.

They lie with their sweet talk: age can be anything but gracious. Nobody would mind it if it were Whistler's mother in a rocking chair, and grandmother at home, baking cookies. Sometimes, it is merely tragic. On the far, shabby side of the Golden Harvest, age has all the earmarks of a dirty trick.

When you were young, acquaintances and family were already assigned their generations as young, middle-aged, or old. It was no surprise to hear that the elderly had gone home to God. It was sobering to see young people reach landmark birthdays, beyond the point of no return. It was a heartbreak to realize that your parents had grown old, becoming, in their turn, candidates for heaven. Many remain gracious all their lives; Hallmark celebrates their beauty with Yeats's *When You Are Old*:

> When you are old and gray and full of sleep.
> And nodding by the fire, take down this book.
> And slowly read, and dream of the soft look
> Your eyes had once, and of their shadows deep;
> How many loved your moments of glad grace,
> And loved your beauty with love false or true,
> But one man loved the pilgrim soul in you,
> And loved the sorrows of your changing face. . . .

The faces do change. In the summer, I say Mass in the New York nursing home where the original Auntie Mame is the most famous guest. She is the dearest soul, well into her nineties. I look forward to seeing her, one of the loveliest ladies in town. On the wall of her room, she has a large poster of Rosalind Russell as the Auntie Mame the theater knows. Hollywood will never make a movie of Auntie Mame in the Village Nursing Home; it's a long, long way from Sutton Place.

Emily Dickinson, in one of her terse little notes from her deathbed, gave notice to her niece: "Called back." That's the way it looks: little by little, one strength after another, we are called back. The sight diminishes; the hearing fails; the teeth get uprooted; limbs turn palsied; the mind becomes childlike. Finally, God requires heartbeat, breath, and soul, and life is over.

Nursing homes, the scenes of nature's demolition derby, try to look cheerful, but the sight and smells of sickness are everywhere. Pink bed jackets can hardly hide the sadness. I've always felt grateful to nurses who made my mother feel comfortable while she was in a nursing home; they reassured her by their attentiveness.

But I wish staff members, especially the younger ones, could be sensitive to the loss of dignity an older woman feels when they presume the right to call her by her first name. Outside an institution, it would be an impertinence to be so familiar without permission.

I'm very self-conscious of growing older. Entering a restaurant, I check the room for the college crowd, the executive types, and the lovely ladies with the pantsuits that glitter and the blue rinse in their hair. Dear old souls know better than anyone, even truck drivers, where the food is best. If I'm staying in a hotel, I take notice of the permanent guests, often widows, who sit in the lobby, checking out faces. I meet them, dolled up and having a drink, in the hotel restaurants with improbable names like the Egyptian Room.

Dinner, I believe, is the highlight of their day. They can keep up appearances until ten o'clock; then, yawning and beginning to fade under the makeup and the jewelry, they retire to their rooms, where they fall asleep watching Johnny Carson. Theirs too is a quiet way of raging against the dying of life's light; their style is a series of rituals to prevent them from visibly slowing down. I cheer them under my breath: "Go to it, old girl. You can still cut the mustard." Illness or injury could put them away in places they dread the most. They keep the masks in place, hiding the pain that could land them in beds in the Happy Valley of their nightmares. They are, with their courage to survive, the heroines of middle-class hotels.

At my age, you begin reading ahead for future scenarios. On the best days, you are optimistic, like a soldier facing battle. You are going to make it through with dignity, but you're worried about the other poor devils who won't be so lucky. On the bad days, you examine every wall for the evidence of handwriting. On the ordinary days, you count your blessings, and sing the September Song.

All you need for contentment is the comfort of a good book, a good drink, and a fine meal; a splendid conversation with friends; peace at day's end from your prayers well said; a quiet sleep through the hours of darkness until the morning; and your dog, delighted to greet you, when you open your eyes.

At 20, you were in a hurry to be on your way. At 30, you felt disappointed when you found it had been more fun to be 20. At 40, you told yourself the lie that life was just beginning. At 50, you are grateful for the contract you think you have signed with the gods. At 60, the wine simmers down to a precious brew. At 70, you will tell everyone that you're not older, but better. At 80, you will shake your cane at the indifference of sunsets and evening stars. At 90, you'll be checking the ground rules for making it as an immortal. At age 100, God will welcome you home to immortal mansions.

This, in my view, is the way the professionals see it, if anyone survives to be a professional in an amateur's sport of merely surviving.

"Have you made your peace with God?" they asked the dying Thoreau.

"I wasn't aware that we had quarreled," he replied.

That's a mood to live and die in, confident that you have no quarrels with God, and that He has none with you. Otherwise, if you are Irish, you piece out faith with fatalism, as in Yeats's *The Countess Cathleen*:

The years like great black oxen tread the world,
And God the herdsman goads them on behind,
And I am broken by their passing feet.

About seven years ago in New York, I was taken to a hospital in an ambulance, wired for sound; the doctors were watching my heartbeat on television, two blocks away. For five days, they put me through the ordinary humiliations. "The weight," they said, shaking their heads. "The blood pressure. The smoking."

I came out of the hospital on Monday. The following Saturday, the cardinals elected a successor to Pope Paul VI. The church bells rang in Rome, New York, and across the world. A young husband and wife came up from Baltimore to take me to dinner. As we stepped out of the taxi in Times Square, street evangelists were playing a hymn, and a black woman's voice soared over the Chrysler Building.

"I sing because I'm happy, / I sing because I'm free;

His eye is on the sparrow, / and I know He watches me."

In the happiness of that day, we felt that God's eye was on all of us. The Church was safe. The city seemed at peace. All three of us felt the possibility that we would live forever.

Two years later, I mentioned the day we heard the hymn in the homily I gave at the young husband's funeral Mass. He died of cancer at age twenty-nine. He didn't leave his wife without a comforter. Three months before his death, a baby was born. The child was a blessing that they hadn't asked for, a miracle that they hadn't expected.

I'm not worried about my health as long as I keep my diet and take the pills the doctor gave me. I try to live by the rules. Unwisely, I suppose, I feel safe from the treachery of being merely mortal.

My return to health felt like a religious experience. I don't know how the others felt. They must have known that in birth and death, some promise from God is kept. The pope we talked about at dinner — who, it was said, died in bed reading the *Imitation of Christ* — would know better than anyone how well God's promises are kept.

I believe God is on my side. The years will break me only if He lets them. When the days dwindle down to a precious few, He will remind me again how He watches over sparrows.

"Men must endure / Their going hence, even as their coming hither:

Ripeness is all. . . ."

Ripeness means the fulfillment of one's allotted years, says the commentary on *Lear.*

At my age, I have the common sense to accept the years as they come, grateful but not greedy. I accept ripeness as all. That way I'm not hearing Time's winged chariot always at my back. I don't have to dread the thunder of great black feet of oxen crashing down on me.

"Make my bed, and light the light,

I'll be home . . . late tonight.

Blackbird, bye-bye."

CHAPTER 11

The Wild Geese

One evening Arlene, my secretary, pointed out some Canadian wild geese flying low in the sky. "They are looking for a place for the night," she said.

"How can you tell?" I asked.

"They're not flying south," she replied. "They fly thousands of miles without stopping, as far south as the Gulf of Mexico."

"When it is a drizzly November in my soul," says Ishmael in *Moby Dick*, "I put out to sea." A sea voyage is Ishmael's substitute for suicide. Wild geese migrate out of instinct, as a way of surviving the winter.

I was writing a letter of consolation to parents whose son had died in unexplained circumstances. It was not the first time I had wanted to comfort a family grieving over an ambiguous death. Once, a friend of mine disappeared. His family telephoned across the country, looking for the young man. After five terrible days, another phone call came: "We have found Michael. He was in the garbage behind the house where nobody goes." I went to Michael's hometown to say the funeral Mass.

Every year the Notre Dame family is faced with the death of youngsters. Youth is not impervious to accident and disease. Every time this campus community breaks up, with thousands of students driving their ancient jalopies over icy roads, you hold your breath until you can start counting noses to be sure all the children have gotten home safely. You can't bless them well enough to keep away mortal illness. Once or twice a semester at least, souls wing off on an eternal adventure, leaving their classmates to figure out the mystery of the absence and silence.

The Lord Jesus, at the Ascension, went back to His Father in heaven so that the Spirit might be sent. When a student leaves to meet His Savior face-to-face, the Spirit of consolation is so obviously at work among the mourners it feels like a time of Pentecost. First, when the bad news comes, there is the grief, heartbreaking and numbing. Next, there is the triduum of waiting, while the bonding in love takes place. Then, there is the holy time, when the campus seems blessed, as American kids with tearstained faces, experiencing grace under pressure, show themselves as beautiful and sensitive. Finally, after the last prayer is said over the body awaiting its burial like the grain of wheat mentioned in the Gospel, all of us begin the rest of our lives, worn out from caring, yet together like a family in a peace without bitterness. The Lord promised: "I will not leave you orphaned. . ." (John 14:18). God never seems closer than when we are saying good-bye to friends who have left us while their day is young.

Graham Greene has a lovely story of the Eucharist called "The Hint of an Explanation." A boy growing up in a small English village is bullied and tempted by the local atheist into stealing a consecrated communion wafer from the Sunday Mass. Later, when the atheist stands outside his window at night, whining threats to induce the thief to hand over the host, the boy for the first time realizes the infinite value of the soggy sacrament wrapped in a screw of newspaper in the pocket of his pants. The story asks: Why does God permit the corruption of children? This child, on the verge of sacrilege, learns the worth of the Eucharist from seeing an atheist's yearning, and he grows up to become a priest. God brings good out of evil. The devil is beaten at his own game. Death is the last enemy to be overcome, says the Bible. In the outpouring of love at a Notre Dame funeral, one is tempted to ask: O Death, where is thy victory? O Death, where is thy sting? A new voice is added to the heavenly choir, and "one of the *Irish*" intercedes for us at the throne of grace.

I had a letter to write. The effort kept me thinking of Michael, who faced some disappointment I was not a part of after he had left Notre Dame. This new death of a young graduate brings back memories of my train trip to Michael's town for the services.

You search for words, for insights, for ways of bringing consolation when you are going to a home that has suffered loss. Without something helpful to say, you can be afraid of facing the survivors. Nothing teases the mind more than the puzzle of death and eternity. Four days before my mother's death, I attended the funeral for another priest's mother. As I listened to the litanies of the burial rite, worrying about my own mother waiting at the threshold of the Father's house, I knew all the promises were true. I was believing the Gospel as though the Holy Spirit had interiorized the words in my heart

and mind. "Come to me, all you who are weary. . ."
(Matthew 11:28). How beautiful it is to be cheered into
hopefulness by faith that leaves you feeling the Lord has
been very personal.

Yet you can't be aggressive in announcing God's
love, as though you were trying to win an argument. You
should not say more than you are sure of; when you finally speak up, you should let God choose the words.

When your back is against the wall, you have to trust
heaven. I had known Michael well, but not well enough to
understand all the ways he was hurting. I could never
have guessed in a million years that he was tempted to
disappear. I was heartbroken to think his existence
meant so little to him. I couldn't attend the wake until I
had managed to deal with my own sadness. I wanted the
peace of mind of knowing that God kept Michael close to
Him.

Michael once painted my picture in an art class. He
wanted me to have the portrait. His family sent it to me
after his death. I was always afraid of the picture because I saw death in that painted face. The eyes were so
lifeless that they scared me. I thought the problem was
with the subject; later, I wondered if the problem was
with the painter. I have never taken the portrait out of
the packing case in which it was shipped. I seem to remember ghosts of sadness in Michael's face; I thought it
was the melancholy of the Irish coming through. His
death will always be ambiguous; appearances were
against him.

I am sure the Shepherd was compassionate, as Michael would have trusted Him to be. Michael had more
faith than most of us who will follow him through the
dark valley leading to the Son. He lived close to God. I
know, like an article of faith, he died close to God, atten-

tive to a better life in a kingdom where the future is always a noonday bright with hope. At my age, being twenty-three would be a gateway to fulfillment; there is the tragedy of Michael's signing off. I regret the restlessness that wore him out so early, but I could swear his homecoming was gracious.

So, after I spent an evening on the train getting my act together, we buried Michael the next morning, and I encouraged his friends to believe, as I believed, that he had made a separate peace. We celebrated him as Housman celebrated an athlete's dying young; ageless now, as in Keats, like the figures on a Grecian urn. His classmate read the Irish blessing, asking that the road might rise up to meet Michael, and that he might be in heaven a half-hour before the devil knew he was dead.

Now, I'm getting my act together again for a different death, for which comparisons are unnecessary, except as homework with which to review the mystery. I read James Agee's *A Death in the Family*. I think of my father's death, and the wake of the former show girl in New York, where there were neither mourners nor a single flower. I left my rosary in her hand because she looked so alone. I remember the old soldier dying in the VA hospital after I had given him Viaticum when it was too late; he stopped breathing while the host was still on his tongue. I think of the old lady who called me to anoint her husband, though he was Jewish, because she wanted him buried as a Catholic.

When I was a child, I felt that there were more births than deaths, and that the Grim Reaper was not efficient enough to get everybody. I was never afraid of death until I read a religious book of my grandmother's telling me I shouldn't be afraid. After that, the nightmares began. Often, when I was young, I waited in a car outside the hospital while my parents visited a relative who was dying of cancer.

I wasn't a morbid child, though "Nearer My God To Thee" was my favorite song. Maybe, because of those early fears which dreaded death as an enemy, I grew up to a vocation which preached the credibility of the resurrection of Our Lord.

The wild geese, knowing the season and the pathway through the sky, set their own course. Michael has rowed the boat ashore. The lonely whistle of a train makes me mindful of faces that I miss.

November, not April, is the cruelest month.

Only The Irish
Know How To Bury The Dead

In New York, a retired doctor died. His send-off makes me wonder why priests are in charge of funerals. Families should be in charge of funerals. If the immediate survivors include six Irish-American Yuppies (five brothers and a sister), dark-eyed with grief like figures from a Celtic passion play, they could have Christ weeping as though He were standing with Lazarus's sisters. The family is from New Rochelle. Ed Foy and the Seven Little Foys were from New Rochelle, only forty-five minutes from Broadway. Eddie Foy would complain of going onstage with his kids, because they stole the show. My equivalent of the young Foys are grown-ups; even when they're acting shy, they steal the show, as good-looking people often do.

For example, saying good-bye at the cemetery, the youngest son, Barry, recited the Irish blessing. He intoned: "May the rains fall soft upon you," and gentle drops splashed down from the sky like holy water on the coffin. "How did he do that?" I gasped. "This isn't grief; it's religious melodrama." Only the great Gaels of Ireland know the magic to use in burying the dead.

I'm one of the ceremonial figures who stage the requiem. The dead doctor's children treated me as though I were his next of kin. The dark Irish are always splendid, as though they were bigger than life. Tragedy makes them as wonderful as giants with royal Hibernian blood in their veins. Their effect on me, gathered with them to grieve in this house of mourning, was overwhelming.

Their mother died five years ago, but the matriarch was there, Deirdre of the sorrows: their ninety-seven-year-old grandmother, the doctor's mother. With him gone, she has neither chick nor child. She told me: "I'm heartbroken, not for me, but for them." These large Irish families, on tribal occasions, come across with such style and class. Emotions are more underplayed in Protestant families. The power of human love followed the doctor into heaven so forcefully that the angelic choirs must have felt upstaged.

The ones who impersonalize death are the priests. I don't wish to knock the priests, poor chaps; but when we do funerals, we're dreary at our work. The problem is that Catholic funerals seem interchangeable. Only the appearance of the caskets changes from one Mass to another, depending on whether they are inexpensive or the best that money can buy. Maybe the mourners, tired from the ordeal of the wake, are happy to see the Church take over. Maybe we've trained our people to expect very little except the essentials from the service, and they've stopped noticing that everything seems canned, especially the music.

The doctor's family planned everything as carefully as though it were a dinner party. Most bodies are hauled from the hospital, to the undertaker, to the church, to the graveyard. The only service the survivors supply are the tears and the money for the bills. Everything else is in the hands of professionals who do it for a living. They want to make it easy for the widow; they take a burden off the family, as needed.

Where the morticians leave off, the parishes take over, with the same organist and tenor or soprano you meet in every church. They use the same three hymns and the Twenty-third Psalm as a responsorial. One of the hymns lately has been "How Great Thou Art," from the Billy Graham crusade. The combination of everything supplies slim evidence for the hope of the resurrection.

The doctor was waked at home from Saturday night until Tuesday morning, and his kids sat up with the body through the three nights. The junior priest came on the last evening to read prayers and say some conventional things, which probably weren't very true. It doesn't matter, because they were highly forgettable — like bad poetry. Listening to him, I felt ashamed of myself for the many times I've been unworthy as a comforter to the pain that was shown me.

After the wake ended, the children, their spouses, their spouses-to-be, the uncles, cousins, in-laws, and other relatives I couldn't identify, gathered on the floor and chairs around the body to plan the readings for the funeral Mass. For two hours, texts were read aloud to see if they stood up to the family's tests. The final list included the verses beginning "Hold the physician in honor" (Sirach 38:1); "[Nothing] will be able to separate us from the love of God that comes to us in Christ Jesus, our Lord" (Romans 8:38-39); a passage from Job evocative of their dad's suffering; and, from the Gospel of Luke, the raising of the son of the widow of Naim. It was a good list of readings. Then we composed the general intercessions.

By the time we finished our homework, it was close to midnight. I had never spent so long with a dead person. I forgot he was dead, and not listening. One of the boys said: "Dad hated the savagery of the Old Testament. He couldn't stand the notion of Abraham standing over Isaac with a knife in his hand." It sounded like something I might say. I felt that God had sent me a sign.

The closing of the casket on Tuesday morning was accompanied by sentimentality setting the mood for tears. I saw a pouch of tobacco placed next to the body. The doctor's elegant Homburg rested on the casket as though he were about to make a house call. They played him his favorite songs on the stereo, including "Margie," which was his wife's name. They said: "One more song, and Father will say the prayer." Bing Crosby sang "When Irish Eyes Are Smiling," leaving me in a condition which made it embarrassing to talk. How could I, with credibility, do a follow-up to Crosby?

I rode to the church in the hearse with two of the undertakers. "Where's Joe?" one of them asked.

"He couldn't get his suit out of the cleaner's," the other replied.

"I always get stuck," the first man snarled. "It would be different if I hadn't told them it was important."

Why, I wondered, did they have to wash the dirty linens of their trade in front of me, as though I were not part of the public from whom they had to hide secrets?

The sons were the pallbearers, together with the oldest grandchild and some of the doctor's colleagues. They

172

carried the casket down the aisle instead of pushing it on the wheels provided. They would have happily borne it on their shoulders during Mass, I think, as a way of showing the world they loved their father. He was their great chieftain to whom all the honors should be offered as though the high king had died at Tara.

Inside the church, a different ball game began, and the family were merely spectators. The priests were in charge of the body. Nothing came off as the siblings had planned. The principal celebrant performed the rite of greeting. In an aside, he said: "What was his name?" Was he uninformed, or had he spent the morning rushing around so much he lost track? It can happen to any priest, but it seemed like a letdown after Bing Crosby.

I could see there had been a failure to communicate as soon as the readings began. Word had never reached the celebrant about the lessons that had been chosen. Concelebrants were doing readings they picked out themselves. The family didn't get to do anything they had rehearsed. I read the Gospel of the widow's son raised from the dead. Then, as the family priest, I preached the homily.

I was not the doctor's contemporary, but I was old enough to understand a man twelve years my senior. His last years were bitter, and I tried to make sense of his anger. The night before, his namesake had said: "Dad could stomp through the house like a Nazi storm trooper. He had this soft underbelly of kindness nobody knew about. All these grateful people have turned up at the door saying: 'Your father knew times were rough with us, so he wouldn't cash the checks.' Your father has to die before you find out what he's like." The same thing was true of Jesus. They didn't know who He was until after He died.

"Anger is a form that love takes after it has suffered loss," I said. "The doctor wasn't old, but life treated him as if he were old. He lost his wife to a painful disease. He was forced to give up practicing surgery because of his age. He suffered sicknesses which he kept to himself. The Lord gives, and the Lord takes away. It is God's way to take back His gifts. It is man's way to rage against God. Rage is one of the final uses a man makes of his divine fire."

I continued: "When the doctor enters heaven, you can bet that God will greet him as one great physician greets another. The timeless conversations will begin with the doctor asking: 'How did You raise the widow's son? How did You heal the withered hand? What did You do to relieve the woman who had been hemorrhaging for so many years? . . .' God will delay him with a show of hospitality like the doctor's own. 'First,' God will say, 'I have a fine bottle of Scotch. Does it interest you?'"

I was not the star of the show, nor did I need to be. Not all of the siblings have their act of faith together. I wanted to help them as much as I could in fitting together the pieces of an eternal puzzle.

At Valhalla cemetery, the new generation of Foys from New Rochelle were again on center stage. Under a gray sky that poured all morning on the raw March earth out of which the first, tiny crocuses were stirring, the women dear to the siblings finally did the readings they wanted to do at the Mass. Then tributes were offered like the phrases of a eulogy. Bob, the eldest, told us: "All his life, Dad gave everything, and got nothing back in return. The hardest thing in the world was to give him anything. The second hardest was to tell him anything. He wanted us all to have an education. We want to report: 'We're here, Dad, overeducated and grateful. . . .'"

174

He told a story on his brothers. At the Jesuit high school, Kevin and Brian got in trouble with the headmaster. As a punishment, he ordered them to spend some hours in the detention room. "Use the time," he said, "learning Frost's poem 'Stopping by Woods on a Snowy Evening.' " Bob said: "He underestimated my parents. All of us kids knew the poem by heart. Kevin and Brian recited it in unison. The headmaster was so surprised that he forgave the jugging."

Brian said: "We still know the poem. We'll recite it for you now." In the charming way of showing off that performing children have, the siblings made their father proud of them by chanting the well-loved verses about promises to be kept and miles to be traveled before sleeping. Worse lines have been used for a doctor's epitaph. Their choral performance was one of those elegant gestures that the Irish make so perfectly, as when young John Kennedy offered the salute to his fallen father.

The sons would have felt entitled to bury their father, if there weren't a labor union which claims the exclusive right to bury the dead. The sons stayed around to make sure the job was well done, though the rain fell on them as they waited. In the middle of the burial, the lunch hour came, and the diggers took off an hour to eat. The siblings didn't leave until the reunion of their parents under the cemetery earth of Westchester was completed. As witnesses, they were faithful to the end.

Later, I congratulated the titular head of the new troupe of Foys for stealing the stage. I said: "Of course you were wrong, Bob." He asked me with his eyes what I meant. "You said that your father gave everything, and got nothing; and that's wrong. He gave everything, and got back giants. I think he was a lucky man."

It's hard, when you're dealing with the Irish, to get in the last word. I'm Irish enough to know when I've found a treasure in the field. The oldest Foy didn't contradict me when I praised him as a jewel. He recognized, I hope, that in having such a family, his father died wealthy. Your father's death not only tells you about your father. Your father's death tells you about yourself.

The Burial Rite

At a Holy Cross community discussion remembering Father John Reedy, one of his friends read an article written by John. The article revolved around a young family who, on a Christmas morning, found that their baby had died during the night. Hearing of the death, John had gone to the house, gaily decorated for the holidays. The parents were gathered with their other small children in the living room. The baby's father was cradling the still, little boy in his arms.

John Reedy wrote: "I had always refused to hold this child, because children seem too fragile for me to touch. That morning, the baby's father was unwilling to give up the body when the undertaker came. Finally, his wife suggested: 'Give him to Father Reedy to hold.' " The father consented to let John take the child. In this way, John, feeling very clumsy and inadequate, was able to carry the body out of the room. The father was spared the sight of his son given to the undertaker's care.

I have never heard a more powerful priest's story than the one John Reedy told so well in his article. Tom and Chris's story is like a footnote compared with his; although, hours later, remembering John's words, Tom and Chris came to my mind. I'm not trying to match John Reedy's priestly experience, sadness for sadness; but there are questions for which I have never found answers.

As students, Tom and Chris were still very young when I married them. Two months after the wedding, she became pregnant. Tom was very proud of his bride, who would be a mother in time for their first anniversary. They were very beautiful; and their youth was part of their beauty, though they were too grown-up to be treated as children. At the wedding, their fathers and mothers, who lived in distant cities, said: "Watch over them." They were too wonderful to be entrusted to me as a surrogate parent. I know how to keep an eye on a growing dog. I wasn't sure what I could do for Chris and Tom. Fortunately, one kept a close eye on the other. I only had to make noises like a relative applauding their success in homemaking.

One Saturday Tom called to ask if he could see me. I was getting ready for the 5:15 Mass in Sacred Heart Church. "Can it wait until evening?" I asked.

"Chris lost the baby this morning," he said. "She's in the hospital."

"Come right over," I said, saddened. I wanted to tell him in person I was sorry, and to apologize for what had happened. I didn't know what had happened, but I needed to apologize. I felt guilty because I hadn't been alert enough to keep them from harm.

When he came, *he* comforted me. Chris was resting comfortably. The hospital would keep her overnight. She would be fine as soon as they got back together.

"You are both very young," I kept telling him, as though I had a right to promise the future. "God will be good to you." As a priest, I didn't want to sound glib, but what can you say to such a disappointment? Tom had not come to ask me for the routines of a consoler.

"Chris was sick in the bathroom," he said. "I took her to the hospital. Coming back, I cleaned up what it was. I didn't know where to take it. I have it in the car." He was talking about the lost embryo.

The Whitman's Sampler box surprised me; I had expected to see something bigger. Mark, Tom's best friend, was guarding it in his lap. It looked lonely and pathetic, but cared about. I didn't doubt it was the best Tom could do. What else could he use for the delicate beginning of a life, so tentative that a microscopic eye was needed to tell how far the miracle had progressed? Tom had so much respect for the contents of that box. He was trusting me to show him how reverence would deal with it.

Tom and I drove to the undertaker's, with Mark as the honor guard in the back seat. I wondered if there was a special resting place for so young an embryo. I have no idea how humble life looks so soon after conception. Only Tom knows the quality of the evidence indicating that nature has started a masterpiece for which God had planned a soul. I believed what he told me, without needing to see for myself. I had respect for the feelings that were in Tom's face: what was precious to him was precious to me. The undertaker would take the Whitman's Sampler box off our hands. If he charged a fee, I had some money.

Nobody was home at the mortuary. Perhaps people don't die on Saturday afternoons. Maybe that's why nobody answered when we called on the telephone. I decided to ask the help of the hospital. The person I talked with was not helpful.

"It should have been left in the bathroom and flushed away like sickness," he said. "That's what we would do with it here."

"I had hoped for something more tender and com-

178

passionate," I told him. He shrugged his shoulders. I'm not trying to build a case against him. Hospitals, I hope, do the best they can. I was in no position to argue doctrine with a hospital. The contents of the box were so very slight. I don't know what theology would say about the disposal of them. God wouldn't think badly of me, I felt, if I used the practical means the hospital person suggested. Chris and Tom would have questions; something so personal to them was deserving of care. I wanted them to feel that love's labor's lost had been disposed of with love. But the matter was dragging on through the space of an afternoon.

I said to Tom: "Let me take care of this. Drive me to the address I give you. Then go back and stay with Chris."

He took me to the home of a kindhearted convert. Neither she nor her husband was at home. The back door was open. I knew them well enough to let myself in and wait.

Her husband came home first. I explained the Whitman's Sampler box, placed for safekeeping on the mantelpiece in the family room. "I would like to bury it here among the flowers, if it's okay with both of you."

He said: "Wait until she gets here. You can arrange it with her." He was not a Catholic. He was patient with Catholics, though he probably thought I was making the kind of fuss Catholics are famous for.

We sat and talked. I wondered if he felt uneasy about the modest little container, once used for candy, on his mantel. His wife came home, and I again told my story. Like her husband, she probably thought I exaggerated the matter. She hadn't been prepared for an emergency like this in her lessons as a convert.

She watched as I buried the embryonic remains very

deep under a bed of chrysanthemums, after she had wrapped the Whitman's Sampler box in layers of aluminum foil so that no animal would be tempted to go digging.

I said some prayers for Chris and Tom and the new soul gone back to Kingdom Come. I prayed for the grave as a place of resurrection, and blessed the box as though it were a tiny casket. Nothing inside the box needed attention from me. If I opened it, I felt, I would find little more than linen towels with stains on them already becoming as faint as ghosts.

We carefully laid a flower or two on the cover before I filled in the dirt. This kindhearted Christian woman gave the burial place its own golden chrysanthemum to make it beautiful.

That day, only she and I knew where the earth was dug up. Now, a number of years later, only she knows the exact spot for sure. I was finished in time to get back to campus for the 5:15 vigil Mass. Nobody has ever told me if I did more than was necessary. I didn't have to be ashamed when I saw Tom and Chris the next day, though they never asked a single question, and I gave them no information on what I had done. I'm sure they felt I had done as much as I could.

I will never be a father facing so dark a mystery as his child's death. Even as a priest I have never come so close to the mystery as John Reedy did. You can forget about a candy box not much heavier than a feather. Tom and Chris won't keep remembering a life so brief it was almost never with them at all.

A Candle Before
The Face Of Christ

Up until about a year ago, I had had Pete's diary for some nine years but had never looked at it. It didn't seem like any of my business, although Brenda, Pete's wife, gave it to me several months after his funeral. Both Pete and Brenda hoped I could so something with it, like telling the story of Pete's suffering from cancer so that he would not be entirely fogotten. The problem is, everyone knows some victim like Pete. He was a Notre Dame law student. He had cancer and died while in school. Deaths like Pete's happen all the time. It was not possible, I thought, from reading Pete's diary, for me to make him unforgettable.

With the arrival last year of Debbie (who worked with Brenda at St. Mary's College), we relived the sadness of January 6, 1975, the day Pete died. I spoke to Debbie of having the diary, and wishing I didn't have it. Now, I've been looking at it again, and it is like reading a series of personal letters telling a story. It is not a story I would have a right to repeat, except that Pete himself, as the following shows, gives me permission to do so.

Under the date of Wednesday, November 21, 1973, Pete wrote: "I've been reading Father Griffin's *In the Kingdom of the Lonely God* and am somewhat inspired. So I thought maybe this would be a good time to get some of my thoughts on paper. First, the only person I really *want* to read this is Brenda. She knows me better than I do and she can understand my moods. If anyone is to do anything with this, I'd prefer first shot be given to Father Griffin. I've come to know him and he writes well and has enough love for his whole body."

It's a shock to read the places where he mentions me, as in the delicate reference to the body which was much overweight.

On September 9, 1973, Pete wrote: "My back has been acting up quite badly again recently. I'm afraid I may have another slipped disc. . . . I'm going to see a doctor sometime this week."

I met Peter the day before the doctors diagnosed his illness. His friends asked me to talk with him because they felt he needed a priest to cheer him up. The second time I saw him, the doctors had just told him he was suffering from cancer.

November 6 • "Well, things have gone bad, very bad. I checked into the hospital three weeks ago today for my back, and they have since found cancer in a vertebra of my back. They are trying now to determine just exactly how advanced everything is before treatment. . . ."

November 14 • "After another series of bad days, I will try to fill you in a little better on the cancer situation. The bone marrow test came back positive — cancer there also. After that hit me, I had three or four very bad days. I felt as though I would not be able to continue. It was very depressing for me. . . . I began cobalt treatment, and my back feels fairly good since then. . . . The intensity of fear is still the same."

November 21 • "Cancer scares me. I still get real frightened when I think I have it. . . . The fear is more that of death than of cancer. The unknown — and uncertainty of life after death, when confronted as a practical matter — is extremely fearful for me. Several things give me comfort however: (1) There must be, has to be, a God who is all-wise and all-loving — if not, why all the brouhaha about life itself? (2) Brenda is so close and so dear to me. She is my source of weekly strength. (3) My family members are firm believers in the power of positive prayer. . . . (4) Many friends . . . are helpful in times of crisis. My faith in God, I think, has been restored in a more or less backhanded fashion. I don't know why — it's just there. . . ." Later: "Thought — maybe if I lived three years well, it could be better than if I lived thirty years poorly."

November 23 • "B. [Brenda], Father Griff, and I are going to offer a Mass of Thanksgiving for all the people who have been so good to me through my stay of now thirty-eight days in the hospital. . . . The Notre Dame law students raised $2,000 for Brenda and me. . . . I at times feel guilty about my being so good about everything — thinking that perhaps I should be acting this way or that — but when you get right down to it, I have to act out the way I feel — even if that is like 'goody-two-shoes.'

"I guess in a way I do feel I can live a good life for the next couple of years — which may be all I have left — but two years is still very difficult to accept. . . . I feel, in a way, that I've always had it in my greater plan to suffer. Somehow that seemed my lot. I was never an outstanding athlete, nor a great campus politician — even though I was president of every group I belonged to at one time or another. Somehow it just seemed that God intended me to suffer. Hopefully, it won't be too much."

December 9 • "What's it like to have incurable cancer? I don't feel any different from anyone else. . . . [But] when one stops and thinks of it — it is very depressing — and that's the struggle. I find myself asking if God exists. . . . For me the question must be answered 'Yes' — all that is now had to come from somewhere — whoever created this world has to be superior to man. Secondly, too many very good people . . . have believed in God — so I take their lead. Also, I have felt close to God often.

Sometimes it seems I can feel His presence with me. . . . I finished the New Testament this weekend. I feel closer to God for it. Some aspects left me mystified. I guess I will never understand fully in this life the wonders and glories of the next. . . . Death is for me at times very frightening and at other times very thought-provoking — almost a pleasant thought. It's frightening when I wonder about God's existence, and pleasant when I rely on my faith in God and Jesus Christ His Son. I know B. has a difficult time — at times — understanding my religion — and I hers — but basically we respect each other's thoughts. . . . I pray that God will help me.''

February 11, 1974 • "Good news has come our way. On February 7, last Thursday, I found out that Dr. Troeger could no longer find cancerous cells in my bone marrow. That of course was like being reborn again. I am praying very hard that the medicine will continue to do its work. . . . Hard as I try, I'm still not as kind and as Christ-like as I know I should be. . . . I finished reading the entire Bible. I am somewhat proud of that fact. It has really strengthened my faith. . . . There is a lot of goodness, truth, and divine inspiration in that work, and I only wish I could put it more into everyday practice. . . . The economy seems to be getting worse every day — as does the Watergate problem. . . ."

March 22 • "I had a disturbing dream last night. I dreamed my father, now dead for over two years, was found to be alive in his casket. In my dream, I remember saying to myself, 'If Dad can make it for two years in a casket, I can surely get over this.' I don't know what if anything it means. I've thought it might mean there is eternal life and Dad has it, and so will I. On the other hand, I thought maybe it means I will get over it [the cancer]. It was such an impressive dream, it seemed to

184

be a message from God. Of course I don't know if it was or not. . . . The Sunday after Thanksgiving I felt God told me I would not die. I would receive three messages, the first to come one year from that day. I'll wait and pray hard. The dream last night upset me.''

April 1 • "I felt stiff and sore in almost every muscle of my body. It worries me some, but not a great deal. I think it's the weather. . . . This little work is becoming a source of consolation for me. . . . In less than a year, I'll need a new book. . . . I've learned, I think, more about accepting my [eventual but premature] death. I can't say for sure, because it may be a passing feeling. Anyhow, I'm not dead yet.''

April 16 • "I had my chemotherapy on Thursday, and can now forget about it for another month. I only wish I could forget about having cancer for a whole month. I can forget about it for hours at a time now, but can't go one whole day without thinking of it. . . . Bill _____, the guy we got to know while I was in the hospital, is having his hip joint removed tomorrow. . . . He has gone through a great deal. . . . It is lonely going through what we have to. No matter how hard anyone tries, the fact is each person has to face a time like this on his own. . . . I worry about dying and leaving B. I want to live so badly and yet I see Bill and others going through so much pain. I'm not sure I could take that either. . . . It always seems a bit difficult to orient myself to reality since I found out I have cancer. I do try to pray a lot, and that does more for me, mentally and physically, than anything else. Somehow I feel God will protect me — no matter what He decides to do to or with me in the meantime. Thus my prayers will continue as long as I am able.''

April 30 • "I spent two weeks in the hospital over

the summer. The cancer flared up. It was depressing — I think in many ways more depressing than the first bout. No one really knows for sure what all this relapse means in terms of long-term prognosis. I feel good except for occasional fever and my blood count. I keep praying God will cure me or give me a long-term remission — but I have to accept His will too." (This was Pete's last entry.)

January 22, 1975 • Brenda records in a pencil-written postscript: "Pete died January 6 . . . of cancer. It was a quiet death. He was in pain, but not complaining. They gave him some shots of morphine, and he just seemed to doze off. He had been in the hospital since December 10. . . . During the day, I tried to assist the nurses: placing heating pads on Pete's arms, getting him ice bags for his nosebleeds and changing the bandage on his nose very often to keep the blood from running all over his face. . . . Pete said: 'Brenda, you always know what I need.' I think those were his last words to me. . . . Father Griffin called about five minutes before he died. I told him how scared I was, and he told me to pray. So I prayed the Lord's Prayer over and over as fast as I could. As Pete's breathing slowed, I clutched his already cold hand and said, 'Don't be afraid, don't be afraid.' "

Pete died during the Christmas vacation. I was in New York, attending a movie, when the usher paged me. The rectory was relaying a message from Brenda in a phone call hours earlier, saying that Pete was dying. I immediately returned the call to South Bend. I have never been so close to death from so far away: it seemed I could hear Pete breathing. As a phone caller, I was an intruder: I couldn't help Brenda from such a distance. Two days earlier, I had seen Pete for the last time. I didn't realize his life was nearly over.

Pete, at the time of his death, was twenty-eight. Brenda was twenty-five. He was posthumously awarded his law degree from Notre Dame. The verse on his memorial card said: "Like a candle our life is consumed before the face of Christ."

January 24, 1975 • "Pete's funeral was much as he would have had it, I'm sure. . . . Many of the readings used were readings from Pete's Bible that he had marked in pencil. . . ."

The Difference It Makes

On a rerun of $M*A*S*H$, Radar left the war in Korea to go home and help his mother. The U.S. Army mobile hospital unit insisted that he go home because his uncle had died, but the whole episode showed how much the members of the unit were going to miss him. Radar left his teddy bear behind for Colonel Potter to mind. Potter, Hawkeye, and B.J. Hunnicutt had tears in their eyes when they looked at the well-worn teddy. The bear had his work cut out for him as a morale officer helping those medics get through the rest of the war without Corporal Walter "Radar" O'Reilly.

I have a musical teddy bear. If you wind him up, he plays the "Teddy Bears' Picnic." My teddy has an inactive life, sitting on the dresser next to a wood carving of Christ crowned with thorns. My dog Darby O'Gill II would take teddy as a toy, if I let him. Teddy has never gone to war, or worn a corporal's stripes. He would be a sentimental keepsake if he weren't so serious a symbol of things that are important.

* * *

We buried Father John Reedy in the winter of 1983. Father Sorin, the founder of Notre Dame, first saw St.

Mary's Lake in the early winter. He wrote a letter to the motherhouse in France describing the landscape as appropriately white in honor of the Blessed Mother. Now Edward Sorin, John Reedy, and other members of Holy Cross sleep under a blanket of freshly fallen snow. The covering is as beautiful as the founder could have wished for December 8.

John Reedy didn't have a teddy bear, but he had a dog: a big, good-natured, irresponsible Labrador retriever named Beau. Beau died a few years ago from the same kind of illness that took his master. Beau lived in a kennel near the steam plant. He got away, whenever he could, to roam the campus. Darby O'Gill II and I have met him on our walks. The two animals would fall over each other like a couple of drunks at a family picnic, since neither dog saw much of other dogs. Trying to lead Beau to his kennel, I got tangled up in Darby's leash and in the belt from my pants — I took the belt off as an emergency leash for Beau — as the dogs wrestled playfully. John Reedy would chuckle when he heard the story. He liked Beau as much as I liked Darby, though I couldn't see why. Beau was lovable for his goofiness; he was never given Darby's advantages; as a result, you never felt like asking him home to dinner. I felt that if there had not been a Darby, there wouldn't have been a Beau in Father Reedy's life. Members of a religious community learn from one another. Darby and I taught John a thing or two, and the proof of the pudding was Beau.

Priests always have "stories" they tell each other. John's favorite stories about me involved eating. One Shrove Tuesday, he said, he watched me put away eleven chocolate éclairs at a party. Actually, I couldn't have eaten more than four or five éclairs, but after many years the truth is forgotten. There is no way of living down the exaggeratons of a seminary story. Another time, John brought me a turkey leg, wrapped in waxed paper. I stored the leg on an outside window ledge to keep it cold until I was hungry. To tell the truth, that turkey leg looked unappealing; even in the cold, I was sure it didn't improve with age. Many months later, John recalled, looking out my window, he saw his offering, wrapped in the original waxed paper.

"Bob kept the darned thing all winter, without bothering to get rid of it," John would exclaim, shaking his head in disbelief.

"I was afraid to touch it," I tried to explain.

John was a master raconteur of these seminary trifles. They were the prime matter of community hilarity, the gospel accompanying the rituals of friendship. Sometimes, you felt nailed to the wall as a stereotype. Often, the legend was more interesting than the character it was told about. You dreaded the disappointment in faces when visitors from the past saw that, as an older person, you were no longer living up to your prime-time reputation.

I shall miss John Reedy, the storyteller who embarrassed me so often. We had a lifetime in common; we were the same age; we hung out our opinions every week in the press; and both of us struggled over the years with problems of weight. When I got down to two hundred and ten pounds and grew a mustache, he kept telling me how I reminded him of David Niven. He suggested I return the compliment by saying he looked like a young Cary Grant. He had never been mistaken for Cary Grant, he said, but he had been compared to Jack Oakie, the actor. He cherished the putdown from the wiseacre who asked: "Reedy, how much do your jowls weigh?" John knew how impressive his jowls were.

The medics of *M*A*S*H* came to attention when they heard the sound of helicopters bringing in the wounded. Those doctors at war faced horror with the rapid exchange of wisecracks, through which their underlying tensions showed. On television, the actors take their text from a prepared script; in real life, the wit doesn't flow as rapidly, though the performers try to be agile with their quips. Community members have a clumsy playfulness with which they try to entertain one another. There are no writers to furnish them with one-liners, but the laughs keep coming. A stranger, hearing us, might ask: What's it all about? It's small talk signifying friendship, that's all. It's a way of not taking yourself too seriously. It's laying aside the mask of the professional for a little while. It's grace, looking secular, that helps you cope. It's love, among brothers, being implicit and shy.

Radar leaves Korea. John Reedy goes home to heaven. Seasoned veterans get a faraway look in their eyes. B.J. Hunnicutt says of Radar: "By now, he must be looking out the window on the plane going home."

Hawkeye answers: "I don't want to think about it." The line belongs to *The Sun Also Rises*. Hemingway's heroes never want to think about it, because it hurts so much. Grace under pressure means having the courage not to whimper at the pain.

John Reedy felt that in my writing I avoided the pitfalls of sentimentality; and though I wrote emotional pieces, I kept the emotion under control. I never figured out if John had a sentimental streak. He made hardnosed decisions in his career as a publisher and editor. As he mellowed into one of our Holy Cross community elders, he made allowances for the emotions in others, though he never became a bleeding heart. John probably understood me more than I understood him. I never needed to understand him, because I never went out on a limb for him, as he did for me in publishing my work.

I have no wish to be his eulogist or biographer; I only want to try to explain the difference that his going makes. I'm glad he thought he understood me, because I depended on him. When he died, I realized how much I depended on his opinion of what I wrote. I would see him at dinner, hoping for his comment on my work. I would wish for the phone to ring with John on the other end offering his praise and approval. He was the most faithful reader I ever had. He was the professional who published the first article I wrote. He knew, better than anyone, what I was up to. He was honest and encouraging and critical. He was the writer who cared most if I succeeded or failed.

Colonel Potter said in his good-bye to Radar: "I'll miss you more than I miss Mildred, my wife. . . . I never thought of you as a company clerk. You were more like a son to me." John could tell me if it was important to keep on writing; now, no one can tell me whom I would believe as much. Part of the ground of reality that I walked on is gone. That is no more of a hyperbole than an army doctor telling a company clerk he's more valuable to the doctor than his wife.

John Reedy was very tender in talking about Beau's death. He didn't feel like replacing Beau with another dog. The big black animal represented John's comic side: a vaudeville act of a man laughing at himself as he takes pratfalls trying to control unruliness. The classic comedians always become victims. John was Beau's victim: the beast always won with his untrainable dumbness, not knowing or caring if he won, because Beau loved John; and John, with his great jowls shaking with laughter, reciprocated the affection. Watching John with his dog, I recognized that when he played the roughest, he was being most affectionate.

The possibilities in life are reduced when you lose people. You keep waiting for a black dog to bound toward your dog, turning an orderly walk into a canine love-in. You keep expecting to see Cary Grant, looking like Jack Oakie, wearing an immense red sweater at the happy hour. You start listening to see if anyone remembers the old stories.

The snow fell yesterday in the cemetery. Life goes on, and so do the Koreas. My teddy bear, good for nothing, watches beside the crown of thorns. Teddy bears are a sentimental touch. John Reedy was right not to have one. Radar should have taken his bear home. There are no teddy bears in *The Sun Also Rises*. And *M*A*S*H*, at Radar's leaving, doesn't tell it the way it is.

CHAPTER 12

Creatures Go A Little Hungry This Time Of Year

Somebody laid out the body of a dead rabbit near the front door of my dorm on a recent wintry morning. The creature must have been run over by a car or hit by the snowplow. Darby O'Gill II and I saw the poor little cottontail on our way to breakfast.

Notre Dame is a sanctuary for wild things. They are very private with their dying, though sometimes one finds a fallen bird. In their innocence animals seem so undeserving of death. Winter is very hard on them.

In Montana alone, a hunter told me, over seventy thousand deer perished from starvation in the winter of 1984. He was arguing that the sportsmen do game a favor by killing them before they die of hunger. I could have argued that the farmers would be merciful if they stopped reducing the size of the preserves by enclosing the land where the deer come to feed. Because of Darby, I'm on the side of the wild creatures. Seeing them hurt or dead reminds me of how vulnerable and unsuspecting of harm my cocker spaniel is.

Winter is hard on people too, but I'm not one of those who suffer. Bundled up like Nanook of the North, I love the winter scene. The evergreens outside my window are vested in white, like surpliced servers in linens starched by cloistered nuns. The trees are like a synod of archbishops robed, as the phrase goes, in ermine too dear for the use of an earl.

Whiteness, Melville wrote, is the color of virgins and the Deity. It is also, in its blankness, the color of leprosy and annihilation. Moby Dick, in his whiteness, was the symbol of many things, like the good and evil in the Calvinist God.

As nature boy trudging through the snowdrifts, I have happier things to think of than the metaphysics of horror represented by an albino whale. I feel giddy with pleasure in my hooded jacket, my fleece-lined hat and gloves, and the heavy boots to keep the frostbite off my toes.

For years I dressed like a gentleman in winter, too proud to wear long johns like a lumberjack. In low rubbers, short socks, and my summer pants, I could have been Adam on his way to sniff orchids in the most sun-drenched corner of Eden.

Now I dress for warmth on winter days, and Darby also wears his shaggy winter coat. The priest and his dog act like a boy and his dog having fun in the season's winterland.

At this writing, I plan to go to California with the Notre Dame Glee Club — with other stops, including Las Vegas, on the way home. My last time in Vegas, I moonlighted as a gambler. I went to the casinos with thirty bucks. I played quarters in the slot machine, losing a little or sometimes winning. Then I hit a jackpot that showered me with one hundred dollars' worth of silver, in addition to some smaller windfalls, until I was two hundred dollars rich. Easy come, easy go; it was the house's money I was playing with. In the end, I lost everything, so broke I had to borrow money to buy cigarettes.

I hung around the casino until sunrise, half mad with the gambling passion in front of the one-armed bandit. Gray-headed grandmothers, winning or losing nest eggs, kept me company. We looked at each other only when the crash of coins into a tray signaled that the machine was paying off a winner.

Our bus left Las Vegas at 7:00 A.M., thank God. Staying longer, I could have lost my soul to the gods of chance. I would have pawned my watch, my dark-blue cardigan jacket, and the Roman collar from off my neck, for the coins with which I could beat the house. Dostoevsky ruined his life with gambling. You can't understand what the temptation is like until you yourself have become just as sick.

I enjoy the excitement of visits to the cities where wordliness gets a bad name. The Apostle Paul, preaching in pagan cities, was full of warnings about staying unstained by the world. Ephesus, Corinth, and Rome were not American cities where the Gospel has been preached for over four hundred years. The Roman Empire offered temptations not so available in Boston and New York. Paul's new little babes in Christ, freshly converted from the daily fleshpots, could easily backslide into pagan immorality.

New York is more remarkable for its churches than for its flophouses, and for its Christians than for its burlesque queens. Los Angeles has its crime rate, and Vegas has its girly shows, yet good Catholic people raise their wonderful families in those towns. Only a fool would try to whitewash the world or deny its wickedness.

However, after two thousand years of grace abounding, Christians living in the glittering capitals of commerce and entertainment are not beleaguered ghetto communities fighting the cults of temple prostitution in Asia Minor. God, who so loved the world, has His eye on the minorities struggling for survival in run-down neighborhoods. Millions pass through the tourist traps, and you can't write off anyone.

Reno, Nevada, is like the field where the weeds grow with the wheat. Atlantic City is like the fisherman's net with the catch that has to be sorted out.

Every hot spot I've ever seen is interchangeable with the fishing villages in Maine in its percentage of the wise to the foolish. The Irish ladies in Manhattan told me of the prostitute in Dublin with faith like a nun's. One of them asked the girl if she was ever afraid walking the streets.

"Oh, no," said the girl, showing the bunch of religious medals she wore. "Our Blessed Mother will take care of me." The Blessed Mother did take care of her, my Irish friend said, because she finally married a rich playboy from Limerick, which it surprised me to hear, because I didn't know Limerick fielded rich playboys.

The streetwalker trusting the saints has her counterpart in a thousand cities more notorious for their vice than Dublin. No town capable of moral miracles should be placed off limits to Christians because it has a reputation for sin.

Pumping quarters into a slot machine until the well runs dry is probably worldly. Meanness beats worldliness as a human flaw. Meanness is a small-town sheriff who beats up blacks out of racial hatred. Meanness is the utility company in January shutting off the gas on an old woman in danger of freezing to death. Meanness is also writing an anonymous letter to the bishop behind a priest's back, hoping that the priest will be reduced to the ranks below the altar boys.

Meanness, rural or urban, includes all the small cruelties that hurt like a pinch. True worldiness is the worship of idols, the setting up of false gods representing power and money. I'd rather be jailed as worldly than as mean. Idolatry mostly limits the stretch of your religious imagination. Meanness shrinks the size of your heart.

I've never kidded anyone about how much I enjoy the glamorous spots, especially when they're expensive, like Caesar's Palace. I go as a poor priest seeing how the other half lives.

I once made the rounds of the casinos of Vegas in a Cadillac limousine on loan, getting supper from the free lunch they offer the gamblers, the only meal I could afford. The next day I went to Disneyland, where nothing's free, and you get the feeling they're deifying the mouse they're singing about. That leaves you more uneasy than the wickedness of the floor shows in the bars.

California struck me as a place to go to in summer when New York wears out, if they could promise I wouldn't have trouble with earthquakes and the San Andreas Fault.

San Francisco is lovely. I've never left my heart there, because I usually catch a cold from the fog or the rain. The little cable cars stretching halfway to the stars, as the song goes on to tell us, remind me of the trolleys I rode to school on as a boy. I have love-hate memories associated with the straw trolley seats I squirmed on as I was humiliated by a girl named Emily. The smell of hot grease from the wheels makes me feel shy and tongue-tied as though I were being laughed at again for being fat. The Frisco native ahead of me looked worried that he was being laughed at for being gay. The little car lost its poetry, hauling so much insecurity up the steep hills.

Rolling stones, they say, gather no moss. I'm afraid you'll think I'm mossless and rootless as a Notre Dame priest who rides frequently into the sunset; a gadabout undeserving of respect, heading back to Greenwich Village for a wedding, twelve days after getting home from Christmas.

I have danced as hard as I could for you, dear reader, to prove I'm not in love with the world in its dimensions as a snake pit. All my worlds are cloisters in which I live like a novice looking for God. I'm too old to be entirely wholesome, too jaded to lose my moral balance in the Taj Mahals serving as pleasure palaces. I'm too big and gray, like an elephant, to get frisky or forgetful of grace.

I've begun the spring offensive on losing weight. All the creatures go a little hungry this time of year. Why should it be different with a gentleman in winter trying to shrink into last year's clothes? I am staying well. Darby O'Gill II is well, thank God. Peter Cottontail left us yesterday. We saw him stretched out full-length on a snowbank. He will not be the last victim of the bitter season.